MIRACLES OF NUMEROLOGY

MIRACLES OF NUMEROLOGY

DR. M. KATAKKAR

JAICO PUBLISHING HOUSE

Mumbai Delhi Bangalore Kolkata
Hyderabad Chennai Ahmedabad Bhopal

Published by Jaico Publishing House
121 Mahatma Gandhi Road
Mumbai - 400 001
jaicopub@vsnl.com
www.jaicobooks.com

MIRACLES OF NUMEROLOGY
ISBN 81-7224-100-3

First Jaico Impression: 1990
Eighteenth Jaico Impression: 2008

Printed by
Sanman & Co.
113, Shivshakti Ind. Estate, Marol Naka
Andheri (E), Mumbai - 400 059.

ABOUT THE AUTHOR

Dr. M. Katakkar was born on 19th February 1924 in an affluent family. He retired as CEO in 1980. Being a son of an Executive Engineer and grandson of retired Deputy Collector and Diwan of the princely state of Bhor, he had ample sources for pursuing his hobbies, career and personality. A commerce graduate from the University of Poona, his lively interest in sports like cricket, tennis, billiards, horse riding and shooting won him many laurels during his college days. His deep penchant for music led him to play instruments like Harmonium, Organ, Sitar and Tabla. Being a voracious reader he was interested in subjects like religion, philosophy, psychology and mysticism. He has read Socrates, Plato, Aristotle, Bertrand Russel, Dr. S. Radhakrishnan, Arvind Ghosh, Upanishadas, and Swami Vivekanand.

In 1970 he developed his own system of Meditation through the study of Patanjal Yoga Sutras. From 1975 he conducted free classes in meditation and gave instructions to hundreds of people absolutely free. His special meditation on Bed-wetting, Developing Regenerative aspect in old age sleeplessness have helped people to solve their worries, problems and false fears.

Articles and Books

His first article "Biological Significance of Palmistry" appeared in 1946 which heralded the beginning of his carrier as a Palmist. He contributed several articles, the most significant being his prize winning paper on "Medical Palmistry". In 1972, his article on "Palmistry in Relation to Psychiatry" was well received by the Medical world at the 24th Annual Conference of the Indian Psychiatric Society. His research work and contribution of several articles has given him the unique status of a Medical Palmist. He is the Author of 15 books.

POSITIONS OF AUTHORITY

a. He is associated with several Astrological societies in India. He is the President of Bhalchandra Jyotividyalaya, Pune and since 1985 is an Honorary Lecturer in Palmistry and Numerology.

b. He was nominated president of Numerology at the "World Peace Conference" held in Delhi in January, 1989.

c. He was also unanimously elected as the President of the "Sixth All India Jyotish Parishad" held on 13th March, 1993 in Aurangabad.

VISITS ABROAD

During his visit to Europe, Canada and the United States in the year 1983, he was interviewed on Canadian television where he explained the nature and importance of palmistry and numerology in our daily life.

RESEARCH WORK

He has done lot of Research work in Palmistry and diseases such as Asthma, Gonadic troubles, Kidney troubles etc. He also visited Sasson Hospital in Pune and did work in venereal diseases and their significance on the palm. He has discovered that born health defects could be seen on the network of papillary Ridges spread all over the palm. The diseases described above have their own whorl like formations at certain locations on the palm. Some sicknesses are also due to psychological behaviour of the person. The psychological root cause also can been traced on the palm from various formations of crease lines on the palm. This is definitely an additional aid to medicine. He has achieved success in his research work.

He has given guidance to several people like—

1. Choosing a right career for the students.

2. In family disturbances so as to join the two minds which are about to separate from each other.

Further Research Work: His Research work is going on in "Palmistry and Criminology". If he succeeds in his work, that would help the police department all over the world.

The aim of his consultations

All his consultations are given with a view to develop the will-power of the individual, to develop his personality by describing to him the virtues he has which he should develop and how he should try to overcome his weaknesses.

His main motive in doing so is to assist people in building up their career; to take them out of their nervous breakdown, to show them the light of hope in their sorrows and help them to recover from their sicknesses by finding out the root cause of their disease.

BOOKS WRITTEN BY DR. M. KATAKKAR

1. Encyclopedia of Palm and Palm Reading
2. Brighten your Future Through Palm Reading
3. Dial your Birth Number
4. Numerology Palmistry and Prosperity

5. Palmistry Marriage and Family Welfare
6. Ready Reckoner of Palmistry, Vocational Guidance and Medical Palmistry.
7. Palmistry of Pictures
8. Encyclopedic Dictionary of Palmistry*
9. Miracles of Numerology*
10. हसत खेळत हस्तसामुद्रिक
11. हस्तसामुद्रिक, सुखी वैवाहिक जीवन व कुटुंब कल्याण
12. अंकज्योतिष व हस्तसामुद्रिक
13. अंकज्योतिष एक चमत्कार
14. जीवनाचे रहस्य-हस्तसामुद्रिक
15. हस्तसामुद्रिक संहिता

*Published by Jaico

ARTICLES PUBLISHED: ASTROLOGICAL MAGAZINE

1.	The Biological Significance of Palmistry		Apr. 1946
2.	Is Palmistry a Science?		Oct. 1946
3.	Practical Hints on Palmistry		Dec. 1946
4.	Palmistry, Pre-destination and Free-will		Mar. 1947
5.	Practical Hints on Palmistry		Dec. 1947
6.	Palmistry and Diseases	Part I	Jun. 1949
7.	Palmistry and Diseases	Part II	Jul. 1949
8.	Palmistry and Diseases	Part III	Sep. 1949
9.	Palmistry and Diseases	Part IV	Nov. 1949
10.	The Truth about Numerology	Part I	May 1951
11.	The Truth about Numerology	Part II	Jul. 1951
12.	The Hand of President Nixon		Oct. 1973

13. How can a Palmist get a place of honour? Jan. 1985

14. Palmistry in relation to Psychiatry
—Published in 1972 in the Souvenir of 24th Annual Psychiatric Society of India.

15. Psycho-Medico Palmistry
—Published on 9th August, 1976 in Jyotish Mahachayan, Calcutta.

16. Study of Numerology Part I to IV
—In Times of Astrology, Delhi, February to May 1987.

HONORARY TITLES CONFIRMED

1. 15-5-1983 "Samudrik Tilak", Phaljyotish Mandal, Pune.

2. 11-2-1985 "Jyotish Mahamahopadhyaya", All India Astrological Federation, Allahabad.

3. 11-6-1985 "Daivadnya Ratna", Andhra Pradesh Astrologer's Association, Hyderabad.

4. 10-11-1987 "Jyotish Alankar", Jyotish Parishad, Mumbai,

5. 13-5-1987 "Doctor of Palmistry", World Development Council, West Bengal.

6. 28-2-1994 "Jyotish Maharnava", Astrological Research Project, West Bengal.

7. 15-5-1994 "Samudrik Vachaspati", Indian Council of Astrological Science, Madras.

AWARDS

1.	10-5-1987	Momento "Grahankit", Pune
2.	10-12-1989	Momento "Date Panchang", Solapur.
3.	6-1-1991	Momento Maharastra Jyotish Parishad, Dombivli.
4.	3-1-1993	Momento Medical Research Institute, Pune.
5.	16-2-1994	Vasudevanand Saraswati Award Maharashtra Jyotish Parishad, Dombivli.
6.	28-2-1994	Bhaskaracharya Award Astrological Research Project, West Bengal.

CONTENTS

FOREWORD

If you make a special study of any subject, from your long experience, cultivation and studious research, you will in the end unravel, to some extent atleast, the so-called mysteries of the subject on which you have so concentrated your attention. To a student of science, what is a miracle to the uninitiated becomes a natural phenomenon with general laws, governed by rules or calculations that all who choose can learn and understand. To the student of biology every leaf tells its own story, every tree its age, every flower its own pedigree. To the student of art, art reveals her mysteries of colour, form, design, and a thousand and one subtleties that escape the ordinary observer.

Since I have been a student of Numerology for a long period, I feel I am in a position to give readers the result of my findings and research.

In this book, I intend to give all available information on the subject of Numerology in a simple way so that any one with average intelligence may be able to follow and experiment with certain rules which will be treated in the following chapters. I am very glad to mention that some of my students who attended my twelve-hour course in Numerology have started independent careers as professional numerologists.

It was only by chance that I came in contact with the Editor of Jaico publishing House at Bombay in connection with the publication of my tenth book. "Encyclopedic

Dictionary of Palmistry". My manuscript was readily accepted by him and he suggested that I write another book on Numerology which would be most comprehensive in all respects. I readily gave my consent.

During our further discussions I happened to ask him his birth date. He told me it was 19th February. Was it merely a coincidence that his birth date coincided with mine? Was it this which tempted him to accept my manuscript and which forced me to accept his request to write a book for him? Did Numerology start playing its role from our very first meeting in developing our relations with each other? The answer lies in the pages that follow.

M. KATAKKAR
79-B/1, Prabhat Road,
Between lanes 14 and 15
Pune-411 004
(India)

PREFACE

The title of the book is 'Miracles of Numerology'—something unbelievable, especially when we are approaching the 21st century. Is there really any such thing as a miracle or a mystery? Is there really any such thing as a miracle or a mystery? Is modern science capable of explaining all the laws of Nature? According to the so-called rationalists there is no such phenomenon which cannot be explained by modern science. I think before talking about a miracle one should be able to define a miracle or a mystery. According to me any mystery is correlated to explanation; it means something intelligible enough as a fact but not accounted for, not reduced to any law, principle or reason. The ebb and flow of the tides, the motions of the planets, satellites and comes were understood as facts at all times, but they were regarded as mysteries until Newton brought them under the laws of motion and gravity. Voltaire has said, "There is no such thing as chance, we have coined this word to express the known effect of every unknown cause." I can quote several experiences from my own life and that of others which can rightly be called miracles because they cannot be explained. We all have heard of Miss Jean Dixon of America whose power of the mind has astonished even the scientists. We know of the French prophet, Nostradamus whose world predictions, even after three hundred years, have proved remarkably true. The famous palmist and numerologist, 'Cheiro' had predicted in 1925 the partition of India. Could there be only a chance that these various predictions have come true? This famous Cheiro has narrated in his biography one incident about the Chinese Tablets. At a very old age Cheiro decided to retire and chose to lead a very secluded life. One day he simply disappeared and nobody knew his whereabouts. However, on one occasion some Russian monks required his assistance and guidance on some very important problem but they could not succeed in finding him. Finally they chose to visit China and consult some experts who were the masters of the magic of the Tablets. With the help of the Tablets, the Chinese experts informed the Russian monks that they would find Cheiro in South America in a cave, and that he would be having a statue of Buddha with him. After a strenuous search, the Russian monks finally arrived at a cave which, they thought, could be the place where Cheiro was residing. They stood in front of the cave and enquired loudly whether there was anybody inside. An old and frail-looking man came out and enquired what they wanted. In order to ascertain that the old man was Cheiro himself, the monks just asked him whether he had a statue of Buddha. Surprisingly enough, the old man answered in the affirmative. Convinced, the monks said 'then you must be Cheiro', and he was Cheiro.

How the system of Tablets could reveal such remarkable information is really a matter of surprise. I will narrate one more example from my own experience. It was in 1980 that I was speaking to an audience of so-called rationalists who could not believe that such esoteric subjects could sometimes perform miracles. I wanted to prove to them that miracles do happen and in fact, there must be some scientific laws and forces which might be working behind these miracles but that the present science has not found out the clue by which they can discover these forces. To prove my statement, I showed them a pendulum and told them with the help of that pendulum, I could answer any question put to me. I started my experiments and the first one was to find out the number which was thought of by an individual sitting in the audience. The second experiment was to find out the message written in a note which was folded and kept before me. In the third experiment, I was given four x-rays which were kept flat on the table; with the help of the pendulum, I had to spot out the defects shown by the x-rays. I was successful in all the three tests and naturally the audience was very much impressed. It conceded that what I did was not a trick but a genuine miracle.

Once we accept that miracles do happen, we have to probe into the possible force that would be working behind such miracles. Once we find out the cause behind it, then the symbol of mysticism the miracle possesses will vanish. However, I will try to explain the possible phenomenon that works behind and the same principle applied to the study of Numerology.

Theory of Numerology

There is the 'Universal Consciousness' also known as 'Chaitanya'. This Chaitanya means tremendous Energy which pervades the universe. We cannot see this force but can feel its existence. If by any technique we can tune up our mind force with this Cosmic Energy or the Chaitanya, we can absorb some of this Cosmic Energy and enjoy its existence around us. There are people who are gifted or have developed certain powers such as telepathy, clairvoyance, etc. because they have the capacity to absorb this Cosmic Energy to some extent. We have heard of the Spiritual Healers in the Philippines. They have mastered the technique of absorbing this universal Consciousness. With the help of this Energy they can cure even incurable diseases. I was informed by a German lady that she was operated upon her chest by these Spiritual Healers, without any knife, without any instrument. She showed me a few photographs taken at the time of the operation. What a miracle! No blood, no knife, no stitches, no anaesthesia. The patient was operated upon her chest, the operation was over and the patient started walking and went home. A phenomenon of the Cosmic Energy.

In support of my theory of Cosmic Energy and of the God Force, I can say that we cannot rule out the idea that in bygone years the secrets were revealed to man by his closer connection with the universal Consciousness. According to the Hindus, the Vedas which form the knowledge of human life and which describe several esoteric subjects, were revealed to man by God. In the Bible we note certain ages when God walked with man. Even in the works of Greek Philosophers we find an age described as one when God talked with man and taught him the mysteries of creation. It all shows that the ancient rishis and saints had the power to tune up their mind Force with the Universal Consciousness.

This Universe exists in the above Cosmic Energy which has powerful radiations. In addition to this Cosmic Energy there are innumerable energies which have their own radiations and waves (Spandana). The vibrational force emitted by every energy has an effect on the radiations of another energy. As already stated, though we cannot see these energies, we can feel them. For instance, we have radio waves or the T.V. waves which in the normal course we are not aware of or of their existence around us. In order to know them we have to switch on the button so that we can pick up the waves. Similarly every individual emits rays and waves and we can know his radiations through the study of Numerology. His birth date is the clue to find out what type of rays are emitted through him. There are nine planets which have greater influence on the human life and each of them has been allotted a particular number. The moment a person is born, he is governed by a certain principal planet and a secondary planet and is governed by the numbers allotted to these planets. He thus starts radiating the vibrations of that number or the plant by which he is governed. His psychology, thinking, reason, emotions, ambition, likes, dislikes, health, career, etc. are all dominated by the number he represents. If this number is in harmony with the number of any other person, he will experience harmonious relationships with the other person. If on the contrary, his number is in opposition to that of his friend, the two can never live in harmony with each other.

We can experience the above theory of vibrations when we are travelling in a train or a bus. We can travel hundreds of miles through the train but we will never develop a friendship with a co-passenger who is sitting next to us if his number and rays emitted by him do not harmonise with our number and our waves. But sometimes we may experience the opposite. We may develop friendship with a passenger who is sitting at a distance from us and we enjoy our journey through discussions, talks and jokes with that person. If we try to analyse the facts, we will find that there was no apparent reason as to why we did not talk to or create companionship with the first type of passenger even though he was sitting next to us and why we developed companionship with another passenger who was actually sitting a little away from us. The answer lies in the theory of vibrations.

It is surprising that this vibrational force (Chaitanya) is existing not only in animated things but it also exists in inanimated articles. Even in our house we prefer a particular chair or a place because the vibrations emitted from that chair suit our own vibrations and there is a sort of harmony between the two. We may visit a garden and choose a particular place to rest. But after some time we may feel like changing the place for a better one. Why so? Because the place chosen in the beginning threw radiations which were not harmonious with our own and which made us uneasy in occupying that place. We therefore, chose to shift to a place with vibrations suitable to ours.

If we believe that there is a moment for birth and a moment for death then as a logical sequence, we have to believe that there is a moment for each and every event in life from birth to death. That is why ancient scholars had a foundation for ascribing to every human being his number in the universe. Not only this, but they believed that numbers have personalities, character and even sex.

Do the stars or the planets influence individual life?

I have heard that some 196 scientists all over the world, after studying the effects of the planets on human life have come to the conclusion that the plants have no influence on the individual life: But my answer is firm and positive. Yes, the stars and the planets do have an influence on the individual being. What is the proof? I give below my own experience.

1. It was in 1942 that two street goers visited my house and asked me to show my palms to them. They were fortune tellers from the southern part of India. After stretching my palms before them, they started uttering some verses (slokas) and then spotting some signs and the lines on the hand. Gradually they started sketching out my horoscope and in about 15 to 20 minutes they prepared my horoscope, an exact one as per the one in my possession. Was it only a chance? Can we prepare, only by chance, correct horoscopes from the palm? I think even if one could cast 10 correct horoscopes out of 100, we cannot say that it is only by chance that these 10 were correct. Science will have to investigate as to why even these 10 were correct. Several other prominent dignitaries

have informed that similar horoscopes were prepared from their palms by persons from the North-East side of India and also from Nepal and Sikkim. If a horoscope can be prepared from the hand, what more proof is required to show the influence of the planets on the human being.

2. It was in 1949 that on one occasion I stayed in a hotel in Bombay. The next morning while I was busy taking my breakfast, a gentleman sitting next to me started talking on the subject of Astrology and in a few minutes described my horoscope to a marked degree of accuracy. I just enquired how he could do it, and he said that he prepared the horoscope from my face only. How very surprising and thrilling! A horoscope could be cast from the face alone. If that is so, how can we deny that the planets have an influence on the individual being.

3. Round about 1945, late Mr. K. M. Munshi, the Congress leader and a dignitary, was the President of the 'Bhavan's Journal', a monthly published in Bombay. He had contributed very valuable and informative articles on Astrology and Philosophy. In one of his articles, he referred to 'The Bhrigu Sanhita' in different parts of India. When he was in the city of Hoshiarpur he came across a pandit who claimed to have an original Bhrigu Sanhita. The pandit referred to a particular page and started reading it. The first sentence on the page was 'You would open this page on such and such a date' (the date of Mr. K. M. Munshi's visit was mentioned). 'When you start reading, you will be surrounded by such and such persons'. The narration was absolutely true. 'The pandit went on reading. After some time he read 'When you come to this sentence, your secretary will remind you of an important appointment'. The moment this reading was over, Mr. Munshi's secretary came out from a neighboring room and reminded him of his appointment with the Maharaja of Kashmir.

Is it not surprising and wonderful? Could it be merely a chance? The three illustrations given above are sufficient to prove the influence of planets on human beings.

There is no doubt that prophecies are often falsified by subsequent events. The reason for this must be sought not in the unscientific nature of this study, but in our ignorance of the causes at work. The laws of biology are not always borne out by subsequent events, but no one would, on that ground, deny that biology is a science. The year of change in life can often be predicted well in advance than the coming of a cyclone. Hence, the claim of numerology to be regarded as a science cannot be denied on the ground that numerologists lack precision and prophetic power. The study of Numerology is just like the study of any other language. Once the grammar is digested, the language of numerology becomes clear and understable.

INTRODUCTION

Dr. M. Katakkar's book 'Miracle of Numerology' is a comprehensive work and covers all available knowledge on the subject added with his own contribution, based on his long study and research for over four decades. This book will serve as an important reference book to all students of numerology and a handy guide to laymen interested in searching for answers to their questions through the Science of Numerology.

Here I must at once pause at the word 'Science'. Is numerology a science at all? is a vexed question. In fact this doubt attaches to all so-called sciences or methods of future-telling. Generally there is a very strong irresistible desire in almost all human beings to know the future. However, to those trained in modern sciences where nothing is accepted without actual experiments in a laboratory, a doubt persists whether the art of future reading can be raised to the status of a science like any other physical science.

This again raises other basic questions. Are future events capable of being known? Are some people able to do so? If they do, to what powers or attainments this phenomenon of knowing the future is related? Are people born with those powers or are there some rules which govern future events and which rules are discernible? Dr. Katakkar suggests that the main methods of future-telling are based on certain assumptions. They are, that the planets influence individual human beings. The planetary position at the time of birth determines the personality of the individual. Again the whole universe is full of cosmic energy 'Chaitanya'. Then there is the theory of vibration through which this cosmic energy travels or is transmitted and each individual is capable of receiving or catching this energy according to his capacity which relates to his personality. A theory is built up on these postulates that a proper study and analysis of these factors can lead to the knowledge of future events in the life of a person.

To support this, Dr. Katakkar has referred to some evidence in his thesis. He refers to the book 'Gift of Prophecy' and also to the biography of Jean Dixon, an American lady, who exhibited powers of clairvoyance since the age of three or four. In the year 1945, when she was about 17 years old, she was introduced to Sir Girja Shankar Bajpai, the then Indian Ambassador to America, at his evening party, Mr. Mirza Ismail Kha, his secretary, asked her 'What about India?' and she instantly replied that Mahatma Gandhi would be murdered. He again put another question, 'What more about India?', to which she replied that India would be divided and that Mr. Mirza Ismail Kha would go to the other part of India. Both the predictions came true.

Dr. Katakkar also refers to the 'World Prediction' written by Cheiro in about 1925, wherein he predicted the division of India. He also claims that the cosmic energy which we can acquire, is capable of influencing both the human mind as well as inanimate objects. He also finds that there are instances where people have exhibited healing powers by mere touch. He refers to the experience of a German woman on whom a bloodless operation was performed by Spiritual Healers in the Philippines. It would not be out of place to narrate here what I had heard from my father about the mind influencing inanimate objects. He was a practising lawyer at Ahmednagar. In about 1920, a few Jain saints who visited Ahmednagar were reported to possess such powers. A demonstration was arranged in the drawing room of another lawyer, Shri Balasaheb Deshpande. Some wooden pins were kept standing in front of the saints and someone in the audience was asked to think of some number from 1 to 9. The saint then closed his eyes and directed the wooden pin to disclose the number; if it was five, the pin would bend and stand straight repeatedly five times and stop. It was just to show that the human mind could acquire faculties capable of influencing inanimate objects also.

At the moment the three leading theories in the field of future telling are Astrology, Palmistry and Numerology. Can they or any one of them be raised to the status of a science? Dr. Katakkar's humble claim is that though it has not been firmly established that Numerology is a science like any other physical science, yet there is ample evidence that several predictions based on Numerology are coming true. Even if 10% predictions come true, there is a case for study and research as to whether this is a mere off chance or there are some rules underlying which need to be discovered. This is the only humble claim he is making. He also invites scientists to conduct extensive and deep research and then either accept or reject the claim of Numerology to the status of a science. In other words, do not accept what he says either as a matter of superstitious belief or reject is as a matter of prejudice. Whether it is a science or not, one thing is certain—that it is useful in life.

Humility is the hallmark of a scientist's lout-look and that Dr. Katakkar has amply demonstrated in his approach in this book. If fans of numerology feel inspired to undertake further intensive research and make their own contribution, the; purpose of this book will be served. I congratulate Dr. Katakkar for his contribution to this study.

B. N. Deshmukh
Chief Justice
Bombay High Court (Retd.)
70, A/1, Prabhat Road
Pune-411 004

CHAPTER 1

HISTORY AND UTILITY OF NUMEROLOGY

The study of numerology is as old as history, and various systems of this study have evolved in different countries from time immemorial. Even though the study has a long history, it is still a matter of prolonged and bitter controversy whether it has any scientific basis. In this book I propose to give some facts and explanations which prove that numerology is a natural science based on experience.

Causes of Discredit

It is necessary for every student of numerology to know why this subject has never been accepted as a worthwhile study. Many causes have contributed to the degeneration of numerology. There is the intrusion of the prejudice of the majority of the educated public who regard numerology as mere superstition and condemn it on the ground that modern scientists reject it. But they should note that in this atomic age, what they consider trivial has been discovered to contain immense power, the atom having gained immeasurable importance. If, therefore, they consider numerology to be too trivial for their attention, I would remind them that many of the greatest truths the world has known, though once considered trivialities, have become sources of tremendous force. Another reason for the degeneration of this science is that though numerous treatises have been written on it, unformulated the tradition and dicta of old writers, whose modus operandi in building up the science was anything but scientific, have been retained by modern authors. This together with ignorant persons practising the study of numerology has brought it into discredit. Thirdly, science has vigorously ignored the study regardless of the fact that occultism formed the basis of scientific discovery, astronomy was developed from astrology, that chemistry was developed from alchemy and that it was through occultism that the path of thought was first opened leading to the development of philosophy and psychology. The taboo which impelled scientists to exclude this study from their research has caused the study to fall almost entirely into the hands of charlatans.

The well known palmist and numerologist Cheiro has stated in his biography that during his earlier years, when travelling in the East and especially in India, it was his good fortune to come in contact with a certain sect of Brahmins who had kept in their hands from almost prehistoric times, studies and practices of an occult nature which they regarded as sacredly as they did their own religious teachings. Among other things, these Brahmins permitted Cheiro to learn certain theories on the occult significance of numbers and their influence and relation to human life, which in subsequent years and manifold experiences not only confirmed but justified him in endeavouring to apply them in a practical sense so that others might also use this knowledge with advantage to themselves and to those around them. The ancient Hindu searchers after Nature's laws were the masters of all such studies but in transmitting their knowledge to their descendants, they so endeavoured to hide their secrets from the common people that in most cases the key to the problem became lost and the truth that had been discovered became buried in the dust of superstition and charlatanism. These ancient people together with the Chaldeans and Egyptians, were the absolute masters of the occult or hidden meaning of numbers, in their application to time and in their relation to human life.

When examining such questions, we must not forget that it was the Hindus who discovered what is known as the precession of the Equinoxes and in their calculation such an occurrence takes place every 25827 years, our modern science after labours of hundreds of years has simply proved them to be correct. How or by what means they were able to arrive at such a calculation, has never been discovered. Observations lasting over such a period of time are hardly admissible and calculation without instruments is also scarcely conceivable and so science has only been able, first to accept their statement and later to acknowledge its accuracy.

The judgement of the Hindus together with that of the Chaldeans, as to the length of what is now known as the cycle of years of the planets, has been handed down to us from the most remote ages. Modern science has proved it to be correct. So when one comes to a study such as his, as to the value of the numbers 1 to 9 which, like the seven harmonies of music are the basis of all music that has ever been conceived, these above stated numbers are the basis of all our numbers and calculations, it is then only logical to accept the decisions of those great students of past ages and at least examine their deductions with a mind free from bias and prejudice.

Apart from the question of mystical associations, the numbers themselves have a very ancient origin. We shall, however, never know the genius who actually invented the numbers. According to Prof. Max Muller, numbers were first invented by the Arabs. But it seems that the Arabs borrowed the knowledge from the Hindus who in their own turn (according to belief) acquired it from God.

The subject of numerology had absorbed the interest of

the most profound thinkers of bygone days. We come across references to figures and numbers in the Vedas and in the Upanishadas. The Chinese considered odd numbers as denoting white, day, the sun, heat and fire. They believed that even numbers indicated dark, night, the moon, cold, water and earth. They incorporated into their culture the Phoenecian alphabets and its sounds and letters as well. Gematrica was the earliest from which revealed the hidden powers of numbers. It ascribed the every letter two values, one of sound and the other of number. The same system is followed even in the modern form of numerology.

For ages the number 7 has been regarded as the number of mystery relating to the spiritual side of things and the number 9 as the finality or end of the series on which all our materialistic calculations are built. We all know that beyond the number 9 all ordinary numbers become but a mere repetition of the first 9. For example, [10 = (1 + 0) = 1], [11 = (1 + 1) = 2] and so on. Similarly number 7 has been considered as the mystic number and we have 7 repeated in the following examples: the seven Devas of the Hindus; the seven Heavens; the seven footsteps at the time of marriage (Sapta-padi); the seven days of the week; the seven Angels of the Chaldeans; the seven Sephiroth of the Hebrew Kabala; the seven thrones; the seven seals; the seven churches.

In the most ancient rules of occult philosophy, whether Hindu or Chinese or Egyptian or Greek, or Hebrew, we find the rule laid down that the number '7' is the only number capable of dividing the number of Eternity. Let this be explained by a example. The number '1' is the first number. It represents the first cause, Creator, God or Spirit. The '0' has always been taken as the symbol of endlessness—otherwise Eternity. Place the '1' and the figure '0' by its side and you get the significant symbol of eternity such as 1 + 0, the 10, and then place as many of these emblems of eternity side by side till you get a figure as 1,000,000. Divide this figure by the mystic number 7 and you get the number 142857.

7 | 1,000,000 | 142857

Add as many zeros as you like and keep on dividing by the 7 and you will only get repetitions of the same 142857, which from time immemorial has been called the 'Sacred Number'. Now if you add this figure you get 27 which when added together gives the number 9.

Pythagoras is a landmark in the history of numerology. The discoveries of the Phythagoreans were numerous. They postulated the ten fundamental oppositions:

1. Odd and even,
2. Limited and unlimited,
3. One and many,
4. Right and left,
5. Male and female,
6. Rest and motion,
7. Straight and curved,
8. Light and dark,
9. Good and evil,
10. Square and oblong.

It was their contention that the Universe is the realisation of these opposites and rests on the equilibrium of these opposites. Even numbers were considered soluble and consequently ephemeral, feminine and pertaining to the earth. Odd numbers were considered insoluble masculine and of a celestial nature. A whole science of number interpretation was developed by Pythagoras. The basic idea of Pythagorean philosophy was that man could grasp the nature of the Universe only through number and form. The four elements: fire, water, air and earth, comprised the holy fourfoldness or tetraktys, to which Pythagoreans addressed their prayer:

"Bless us, divine number, thou who generatest gods and men! O holy, holy tetraktys, thou that containest the root and the source of eternally flowing creation! For the divine number begins with the profound, pure unity until it comes to the holy four; then it begets the mother of all, the all comprising, the all-abounding, the first born, the never swerving, the never tiring holy ten, the keyholders of all."

Pythagoras established a study centre at Crotona where this subject was taught and oaths of secrecy were taken. Later on Plato accepted the qualities assigned to numbers by Pythagoras.

According to the wisdom of ancient sages the world came into being through 'sound, harmony, vibration and the spoken word'. 'Quaballah' is one of the oldest forms of knowledge. The meaning of Quaballah is "received from god". This Quaballah deals with Numerology which is but one of its subjects. The teaching of Quaballah has been referred to as 'the inner teaching of the Mosaic Law. Tradition says that God taught it to a school of angels who in turn taught it to Adam and to Noah.

So much importance was placed on the sound and vibrations of the name that we are told it has been an old custom of the Jews to change the name of persons at the point of death so as to effect better conditions and aid the sufferer on the road to recovery. The teaching of this philosophy was that in order to annul destiny's evil decree, prayer, charity, change of name and change of actions were necessary.

Utility of the study of Numerology

Every experience is knowledge and therefore useful in everyday life. We have seen above that for thousands of years this subject has been practised in all countries and at all times and even scientists and the educated people have been taking valuable tips from the scholars of this subject at critical moments in their lives. Even the topmost political leaders who mould the destiny of their nations, take advice from astrologers and numerologists and enquire about their own destiny. It is a matter of great interest that during the second world war, Hitler used to consult his astrologer on many occasions. However, when the astrologer found that after getting repeated success in battles, Hitler had started ignoring his hints, he stopped serving him. He then approached the then British Prime Minister Mr. Winston Churchill who consulted the astrologer till the end of the war. It is said that the great Emperor Napoleon Bonaparte used to spell his name as Napoleone Buonapart. But on the advice of a numerologist he omitted the letters 'e' and 'u' from his name and heightened the power of his personality, and became the Emperor.

If by our study of numbers, we are able to find out the laws of nature that affect our lives, we shall be more happy, healthy and successful in life if we are in harmony and move with such laws. If we can increase the power of our number by constantly repeating it and making use of that number in each and every action, we can absorb the cosmic energy and benefit by that energy. It will add to our personality. We have several self-improvement goals, such as, improving our personality, improving our speech, improving our prospects in business etc., similarly the study of numerology will improve our lives by increasing the vibrational force of our personality and lessening the intensity of our difficulties and obstructions.

I take the liberty to narrate one or two instances from my experience which will convince the readers of the practical utility of the study on Numerology.

A few years ago a businessman manufacturing electronic goods approached me and told me that he was trying for a collaboration with another big industry, but somehow, the actual documentation was being postponed and the contract could not be finalised. After working out his birth date and the name, I suggested that he make a small change in his name and add one more 'a' to his name. In order to get quick results, I suggested he should go on writing his name with the new addition, at least twenty to thirty thousand times. He could do so by writing it on a piece of paper for about ten minutes every day. Surprisingly enough, his long awaited contract was finalised within three weeks.

On another occasion, a relative of mine had complained about her two-year old daughter who was extremely hot tempered and would go on crying for hours together. The daughter was a problem to the parents and they had to divert all their attention to her. I studied the birth-date and the name of the daughter and found that there was a disparity in the vibrations created by the birth-date and the name. I suggested that she change her name and repeat it as least twenty to thirty thousand times. After about five weeks, there was a remarkable change in the temper of the daughter and she showed considerable improvement in her behavior.

One of my friends is governed by the number 4 and it is his experience that this number 4 is haunting him. He hardly escapes the influence of number 4 in the events in his life/ He therefore decided to take full advantage of this number. Once he visited Las Vegas and found that a particular day was fully affected by number 4 and he decided to try his luck in gambling at the casino. He wanted to occupy chair number 4 and wanted to start the game at 4 pm. He played with his $40 and at the end he came out successfully with $4,000.

People have often come to me for suggesting to them a suitable name before they start an industry or print their letter-heads. Alongwith the study of Numerology, lucky colours and lucky stones are also recommended. The theory of vibrations is equally applicable to colours or precious stones and therefore these aspects also have been dealt with in this book. This is a study of psychoanalysis and by this study we are able to understand ourselves as well as others in a better way. We know our abilities, virtues and our drawbacks. We can take advantage of our ability and try to come over our drawbacks. This will brighten our future and make us successful in life. Experience shows that sometimes a radical change in life can take place and an ordinary life can have a turning point. An ordinary person can reach heights undreamt of.

Numerology as explained in these chapters is equally helpful in selecting a marriage partner. In the normal course, the horoscopes of the two are compared in order to find out their compatibility. But interpreting horoscopes is a matter of deep study and its place can be taken by the study of numerology. I have prepared charts for the date as well as for the months which indicate our friends and our affinities. These charts will be helpful in selecting a partner in life so as to ensure a happy married life.

Numerology is equally useful in selecting the proper and lucky day for a particular act. It also helps in tracing out articles that are lost.

Lawyers and salesmen who must cater to the general public will find Numerology invaluable, a big and important improvement over ordinary business psychology, employment managers will find it an aid to setting dates for appointments and in naming locations of assignments. We can also learn from this study in what locality or community we vibrate best and with whom we should or should not associate both for our own good and for the good of others.

In short, the study of Numerology can assist in solving many of our problems and in leading us to the path of success.

CHAPTER 2

THE IMPORTANCE OF NUMBERS

a. Basic facts about Numbers

i. LUCKY AND UNLUCKY NUMBERS

Quite often, a question is asked as to whether there are certain numbers which are considered lucky and certain others as unlucky. In the study of Numerology there are no lucky or unlucky numbers as such. What may be a lucky number for one person may not be so for another person. It all depends upon what number one is governed by. Even then, in the past, some people have thought of certain numbers as unlucky. For instance, the Romans regarded *even* numbers as unlucky. An independent importance is given to number 3. Most of the faiths of the world have recognised a trinity such as, Brahma-Vishnu-Mahesh; Horos-Isis-Osiris; Dharma-Artha-Kama; Satva-Raja-Tama. From the earliest times sacrifices and vows have been repeated three times. There is a common superstition that events take place in threes and that the third time will be lucky. There is a story of Jesus. At the age of 12, Jesus was lost for 3 days. At 30 he took up his 3 year's mission. He accepted 12 apostles of whom one was to betray him for 30 pieces of silver and another deny him 3 times. It is still the custom to bury the dead three days after the death. In the Church, the banns of marriage are read three times. In Mohammedan religion, the divorce takes place on the utterance of the word 'Talakh' three times. Pythagoras and Aristole based their philosophy on a triplet: Creation, Formation and Destruction.

Similarly a separate importance is given to number 7 as has been seen in the first chapter.

ii. ODD AND EVEN NUMBERS

We have also considered in the first chapter the significance of Odd and Even numbers, and found that Odd numbers were considered masculine, insoluble and of celestial nature whereas, the Even numbers were considered as feminine and pertaining to Earth. In the study of Numerology, there is a system of Pyramids, which I will deal with later on in these pages. According to the system of Pyramids, a question is asked spontaneously and instantaneously which is then expressed in numbers. These numbers are added and written in shape of a Pyramid. Finally, there remains a single number. If that number is odd, it shows success; if it is even, it shows failure. If the question is about a child, whether a woman would beget a son or a daughter, an even number foretells a daughter and an odd number indicates a son.

iii. FEAR OF NUMBER 13

There are opposite views about the significance of this number. In the West, this is not a lucky number. It is because this number is associated with the fact that 13 sat down to the Last Supper, and one of them died in a year. The psychological impact of this occurrence is so much on the human mind that it is said that even in some of the hospitals in the West, a 13th bed is avoided, though tactfully.

There is another cause as to why there is a fear of this number. The occult symbolism that stood for number 13 was represented by a mystic picture of 'A skeleton with a scythe in its bony hands reaping down men.' Nobody could understand its real significance and it was considered as an unlucky number. However, it can have an unlucky significance if the number 13 emerges only by chance, that is to say, if a number of people are invited to supper, and only 13 remain present, then it may be a bad omen. Accordingly to the Hindu system of prediction, there are eight methods with the help of which we can predict future events. In that system, there is a significance attached to the phenomenon 'Lakshana' (omen). These eight methods are as under:

1. *Anga* (Limbs):
   This explains the significance of the body from the top of the head to the bottom of the feet.

2. *Swapna* (Dreams):
   This method explains the interpretation of the dreams, in relation to the future.

3. *Swar* (Sound):
   This system foretells the significance of the various sounds of creatures and birds. For instance, crowing of a cock, crying of a dog, noise of a lizard, etc.

4. *Bhomi* (Attitude):
   This has reference to the behaviour of a person, his gait, style of walking, sitting, talking, etc. and their relation to future events.

5. *Vyanjana* (Marks on the body):
   Certain signs on the body which are since birth, such as mole, spots, etc.

6. *Lakshana* (Omen):
   Winking of the eye-lids, scratching of the left hand or the right hand, etc.

7. *Utpath* (Phenomena like earth quakes, volcano).
8. *Anthriksha* (Sky appearance of comets, circle around the Moon).

As regards *Lakshana* (Omen) I will narrate my own experience.

Nature gives us warning of coming dangers. We have to understand that it is a warning and try to avoid the danger. I know of a person who got up one fine morning and decided to take a jolly trip to a neighboring village. He asked his wife to go with him. But due to some other commitments, the wife was reluctant to join him. This was the first warning not to take the trip. Thereafter, he went to his garage and found that one of the wheels of his car had burst. This was the second warning but he did not take notice of it. He replaced the wheel and took out the car. Since his wife was not willing to accompany him, he wanted to contact a friend for a happy ride. On his way to his friend, the fuel in the car gave way and he had to leave the car on the road and go to collect petrol. This was the third warning. Finally he got his friend to join him and soon found himself on the highway. Within half an hour the replaced wheel burst all of a sudden and he lost control over his car which left the road and went into a ditch. There were a few fractures in his legs and the back and he had to spend some three months in the hospital. This is how we ignore the warnings given to us by nature. According to *Hindu shastras*, *'Lakshana'* gives us an indication of future events.

iv. SIGNIFICANCE OF NUMBER '0'

'0' stands for infinity, the Infinite boundless being, the origin of all things, the *Brahmanda* or the egg of the Universe, the solar system in its entirely. Therefore it signifies universality, cosmopolitanism. It also stands for negation and limitation. Thus '0' means the infinitely great and the infinitely small. It means the circle of infinity and the point at the centre, the atom.

v. SPECIAL CHARACTERISTICS OF NUMBERS '4' AND '8'

All those born on 4th, 13th, 22nd and 31st of any month are dominated by the number 4, and all those born on 8th, 17th and 26th of any month are dominated by the number 8. It has been observed in the study of numerology that those who are governed by these two numbers are always haunted by them. These two numbers go on establishing their dominance in the career of the individual and these numbers will always recur on several important occasions. For instance, supposing a man starts writing an important letter, he will find that the date on which he is writing the letter is the 4th, 13th or 22nd or 31st of the month. In case he is dominated by the number 8, the date will be 8th, 17th or 26th of the month. If such an individual enters into a contract or purchases a new car or a house, the date will usually be in the series of 4 or 8. As a general rule, numbers 4 and 8 indicate delays and difficulties in life though they have other positive and good qualities too. If the individuals governed by either of these two numbers or both, find that the events that have taken place on these dates have created hardship or obstacles in their progress, it is better to avoid these dates and numbers while deciding upon important moves. In that case a person governed by number 4 should try to take his decisions on number 1 or 2 and a person dominated by number 8 should take his actions on a 3 or 7 series.

As regards number 4, I have narrated an experience in the first chapter that the person could get $4,000 after making full use of his number 4. On one occasion he wanted to prove his conviction to one of his friends and both of them decided to go to a cinema show. His friend purchased the tickets and the ticket numbers were 13 and 14. He purposely occupied the seat No. 14 (which makes a total of 5) and asked his friend to occupy the chair with No. 13 (making a 4). After about half an hour a lady sitting behind requested my friend to exchange the seats if possible because the picture was not quite visible to her. He therefore changed the seat and occupied the chair No. 13 and his friend occupied the chair No. 14. Thus even against his wishes he was forced to occupy a chair the number of which was 4 when reduced to a single digit.

It is my experience that if the number 4 is dominant in the case of ladies, i.e. if they are born on 4th, 13th, 22nd and 31st of any month, they are of great will power, uneasy and very dominant. They are headstrong and sometimes even cruel. They always make others dance to their tune. This is more so if they are born during the period of Mars and on the 22nd November and even 22nd December. I request my readers to compare my experience with their own experience.

For the delay shown in by numbers 8, please read the interesting case given in the chapter on number 8.

It is also my experience that those who are born in April or August (4th and 8th month) and also have dates in the series of 4 and 8 have children who are dominated by either of the two numbers. At least one or two children out of the 4 are born in these series.

More information about the significance of Numbers

Every number has a certain power which is not expressed by the figure or symbol employed to denote quantity only. This power rests in an occult connection existing between the relations of things and the principles in nature of which they are the expression.

Number 1: It denotes individuality and possible egotism, self-reliance, affirmation and distinction.

Number 2: It shows relationship, psychic attraction, emotion, sympathy or antipathy, doubt and vacillation.

Number 3: This is the number of expansion, increase, intellectual capacity, riches and success.

Number 4: It speaks of realisation, property, possession, credit and position and materiality.

Number 5: It stands for reason, logic, ethics, travelling, commerce and utility.

Number 6: It expresses cooperation, marriage, reciprocity, sympathy play, art, music and dancing.

Number 7: It indicates equilibrium, contracts, agreements, treaties, bargains, harmony and discord.

Number 8: This number represents reconstruction, death, negation, decay, loss, extinction and going out.

Number 9: It shows penetration, strife, energy, enterprise, dividing anger and keenness.

b. Affinity of Numbers

i. NUMBERS, THEIR FRIENDS AND PLANETS

There are 9 planets and they are represented by 9 different numbers. In the birth date, there are only numbers which represent planetary influences. The planets as well as the numbers have harmonious vibrations with certain other planets and numbers.

Following is the relation between planets and the numbers:

Number	*Planet*	*Friendly Number*	*Unfriendly Numbers*
1	Sun	1, 3, 4, 5, 7, 9	2, 6, 8
2	Moon	2, 4, 6, 9	1, 3, 5, 7, 8
3	Jupiter	1, 3, 5, 6, 7, 8, 9	2, 4
4	Uranus	1, 2, 4, 5, 7, 8, 9	3, 6
5	Mercury	1, 3, 4, 5, 7, 8	2, 6, 9
6	Venus	2, 3, 6, 9	1, 4, 5, 7, 8
7	Neptune	1, 3, 4, 5, 7, 8,9	2, 6
8	Sturn	3, 4, 5, 7, 8	1, 2, 6, 9
9	Mars	1, 2, 3, 4, 6, 7, 9	5, 8

There is another system known as the Unit Method by which the harmonies of numbers are as under:

1 Vibrates to 9; attracts 4 and 8; disagrees with 6 and 7. It is passive to 2, 3 and 5.

2 Vibrates to 8; attracts 7 and 9; disagrees with 5. It is passive to 1, 3, 4 and 6.

3 Vibrates to 7; attracts 5, 6 and 9; disagrees with 4 and 8. It is passive to 1 and 2.

4 Vibrates to 6; attracts 1 and 8; disagrees with 3 and 5. It is passive to 2, 7 and 9.

5 Vibrates to 5; attracts 3 and disagrees with 2 and 4. It is passive to 1, 6, 7, 8 and 9.

6 Vibrates to 4; attracts 3 and 9; disagrees with 1 and 8. It is passive to 2, 5 and 7.

7 Vibrates to 3; attracts 2; disagrees with 1 and 9. It is passive to 4, 5, 6 and 8.

8 Vibrates to 2; attracts 1 and 4; disagrees with 3 and 6. It is passive to 5, 7 and 9.

9 Vibrates to 1; attracts 2, 3 and 6; disagrees with 7. It is passive to 4, 5 and 8.

i. A number vibrating to another shows that there is considerable mutual attraction and the marriage will be very favourable.

ii. A number that attracts another shows that the two people are well suited to each other.

iii. A number that disagrees with another shows that the union will call for a great deal of diplomacy, if it is to be attended with any measure of success.

iv. Where a number is passive, it merely means that numerology offers no opposition, there being no outstanding influence for good or bad.

v. If the two numbers are alike, it is a foregone conclusion that the union will be very favourable.

C. The significance of Numbers

The significance of numbers according to Pythagorean is as under:

1 Impulse, passion, ambition, intention.

2 Death, fatality, destruction.

3 Religion, faith, destiny.

4 Solidity, strength, power.

5 Marriage, pleasure, joy, happiness.

6 Perfection of work.

7 Rest, happiness, equilibrium, freedom.

8 Protection, justice.

9 Grief, anxiety, maiming, imperfection.

10 Reason, success, aspiration.

11 Discord, offence, deceit, punishment.

12 A fortunate writing, a town or city.

13 Wickedness, wrong.

14 Sacrifice, loss.

15 Virtue, culture, integrity, goodness.

16 Luxury, sensuality, good fortune.

17 Misfortune, disregard, oblivion.

18 Miserliness, hardness, tyranny.

19 Foolishness, insanity.

20 Wisdom, severity, melancholy.

21 Mystery, fecundity, production.

22 Chastisement, penalty, hurt.

23 Revolt, bigotry, prejudice.

24 Travelling, exile inconstancy.

25 Intelligence, progeny.

26 Benevolence, charity.

27 Bravery, heroism, daring.

28 Gifts, tokens, omens.

29 News, a chronicle.

30 Marriage, celebrity, celebration.

31 Goodness, aspiration, publicity.

32 Marriage, consummation.

33 Gentleness, virtue, grace.

34 Suffering, retribution, penalties.

35 Health, peace, competence.

36 Intuition, genius.

37 Fidelity, marital joys.
38 Malice, greed, deformity.
39 Laudation, honour.
40 Wedding, feasting, holiday.
41 Disgrace, scandal, abuse.
42 Short life, misery.
43 Worship, religion, sanctuary.
44 Elevation, kingship, ovation, magnificence.
45 Progeny, population.
46 Fecundity, fruitfulness.
47 Long life, happiness.
48 Justice, judgement, a court.
49 Avarice, cupidity.
50 Freedom, release, easiness.
60 Marital bereavement.
70 Initiation, science, integrity, virtue.
80 Protection, recovery, convalescence.
90 Affliction, disfavour, error, blindness.
100 Divine favour, ministry of angles.
200 Hesitation, fear, uncertainty.
300 Philosophy, knowledge, protection.
400 Long journeys, pilgrimage, exile.
500 Holiness, sanctity, selection.
600 Perfection, perfect performance.
700 Might, dominion, authority.
800 Conquest, empire, power.
900 Strife, war, feuds, eruptions.
1000 Mercy, charity, sympathy.

Important: The Pythagorean system mainly applies to the vibrations of names. According to this method each letter is ascribed a particular number and the final total of the numbers in a name has its own significance. More information about this method is given in Chapter 16, 'What's in a Name?'.

This significance of numbers according to the Tarot system is as under:

The Tarot System

The precise origin of Tarot cards is obscure. But probably it originated in Egypt and amongst gypsies. From there it spread to Europe and other countries. A true Tarot is a symbolism. It contains 78 cards divided into two main groups:

22 Major Arcane Cards;

56 Lesser Arcane Cards.

The 22 Major Arcane or emblematic cards are also referred to as trumps (*atouts* in French, *atutti* or *triomfi* in Italian) signifying 'above all'. These 22 symbols have an occult significance as under:

1 *The Magician:*
Skill, diplomacy, address; sickness, pain, loss, disaster; self-confidence, will; the Querente, if male.

Reversed: Physician, mental disease, disgrace

2 *The High Priestess:*
Secrets, mystery, the future as yet unrevealed; the woman who interests the Querente, if male. If the Querente is female, silence, tenacity, wisdom, science.

Reversed: Passion, moral or physical ardour, conceit, surface knowledge.

3 *The Empress:*
Fruitfulness, action, initiative, length of days, the unknown, also difficulty, doubt, ignorance.

Reversed: Light, truth, the unraveling of involved matters, public rejoicings.

4 *The Emperor:*
Stability, power protection, a great person, aid, reason, conviction.

Reversed: Benevolence, compassion, credit, also confusion to enemies, obstruction, immaturity.

5 *The Hierophant or the Master:*
Marriage alliance, captivity, servitude, mercy and goodness, inspiration, the man to whom the Querente has recourse.

Reversed: Society, good understanding, concord, over kindness, weakness.

6 *The Lovers:*
Attraction, love, beauty, trials overcome.

Reversed: Failures, fooling designs.

7 *The Chariot:*
Help, providence, also war, triumph, presumption, vengeance, trouble.

Reversed: Riot, quarrel dispute, litigation, defeat.

8 *Strength:*
Power, energy, action, courage, magnanimity.

Reversed: Despotism, abuse of power, weakness.

9 *The Hermit:*
Prudence, dissimulation, roguery, corruption.

Reversed: Concealment, disguise, policy, fear, unreasoned caution.

10 *Wheel of Fortune:*
Destiny, fortune, success, luck, felicity.
Reversed: Increase, abundance, superfluity.

11 *Justice:*
Equity, righteousness, probity, executive.
Reversed: Law in all departments, bigotry, bias, excessive severity.

12 *The Hanged Man:*
Wisdom, circumspection, discernment, trials, sacrifice, intuition, divination, prophecy.
Reversed: Selfishness, the crowd, body politic.

13 *Death:*
End, mortality, destruction, corruption.
Reversed: Inertia, sleep, lethargy, petrifaction, somnambulism.

14 *Temperance:*
Economy, moderation, frugality, management, accommodation.
Reversed: Things connected with churches, religions, sects, the priesthood; also disunion, unfortunate combinations, competing interests.

15 *The Devil:*
Ravage, violence, vehemence, extraordinary efforts, force, fatality, that which is predestined but not for this reason evil.
Reversed: Evil fatality, weakness, pettiness, blindness.

16 *The Tower:*
Misery, distress, indigence, adversity, calamity, disgrace, deception, ruin.
Reversed: Oppression, imprisonment.

17 *The Star:*
Loss, theft, privation, abandonment.
Reversed: Arrogance, haughtiness, impotence.

18 *The Moon:*
Hidden enemies, danger, calumny, darkness, terror, deception, error.
Reversed: Instability, inconstancy, silence, lesser degrees of deception and error.

19 *The Sun:*
Material happiness, fortunate marriage, contentment.
Reversed: The same as above but in lesser degree.

20 *The Last Judgement:*
Change of position, renewal, outcome.
Reversed: Weakness, pusillanimity, simplicity, also deliberation, decision, sentence.

21 *Zero The Fool:*
Folly, mania, extravagance, intoxication, delirium, frenzy.
Reversed: Negligence, absence, distribution, carelessness, apathy, nullity, vanity.

22 *The World:*
Assured success, voyage, route, emigration, flight, change of place.
Reversed: Inertia, fixity, stagnation, permanence.

Further explanation of the above Tarot interpretation will be given in Chapter 18. This system is based on the symbols of cards. *Reversed* means the card is upside down.

d. Months and their Planets

Each month is dominated by a particular planet and the

month has an affinity or attraction towards certain other months. These months and planets are as under:

Month	*Planet*	*Months of Affinity*
January	Saturn	January, April, July, October.
February	Saturn	February, May, August, November.
March	Jupiter	March, June, September, December.
April	Mars	April, July, October, January.
May	Venus	May, August, November, February
June	Mercury	June, September, December, March.
July	Moon	July, October, January, April.
August	Sun	August, November, February, May.
September	Mercury	September, December, March, June.
October	Venus	October, January, April, July.
November	Mars	November, February, May, August.
December	Jupiter	December, March, June, September.

SQUARE OF AFFINITY

From the above table of affinity, we observe that each month has an affinity towards every third month. Thus, the month January has an affinity towards the months of April,

July, October and the month January itself. This forms a square which is represented as follows:

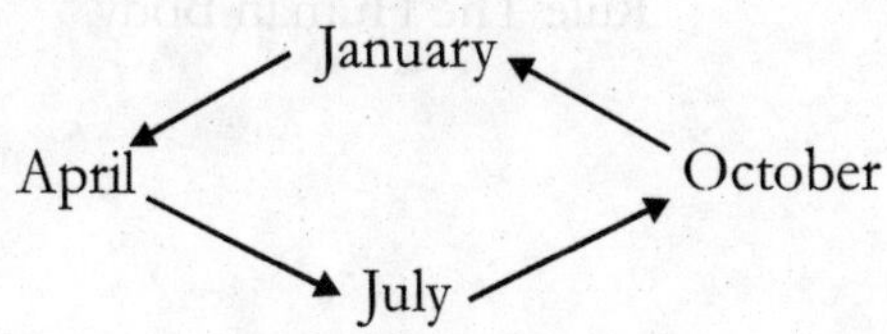

e. Rasis (Zodiacal Signs) and their Periods

	Rasis	*Period*
1.	Aries (Mesh)	21st March to 20th April
2.	Taurus (Vrishabha)	21st April to 20th May
3.	Gemini (Mithun)	21st May to 20th June
4.	Cancer (Kark)	21st June to 20th July
5.	Leo (Simha)	21st July to 20th August
6.	Virgo (Kanya)	21st August to 20th September
7.	Libra (Tula)	21st September to 20th October
8.	Scorpio (Vrischika)	21st October to 20th November
9.	Sagittarius (Dhanu)	21st November to 20th December
10.	Capricorn (Makara)	21st December to 20th January
11.	Aquarius (Kumbha)	21st January to 20th February
12.	Pisces (Meena)	21st February to 20th March

How Numbers And Zodiacs Rule The Human Body

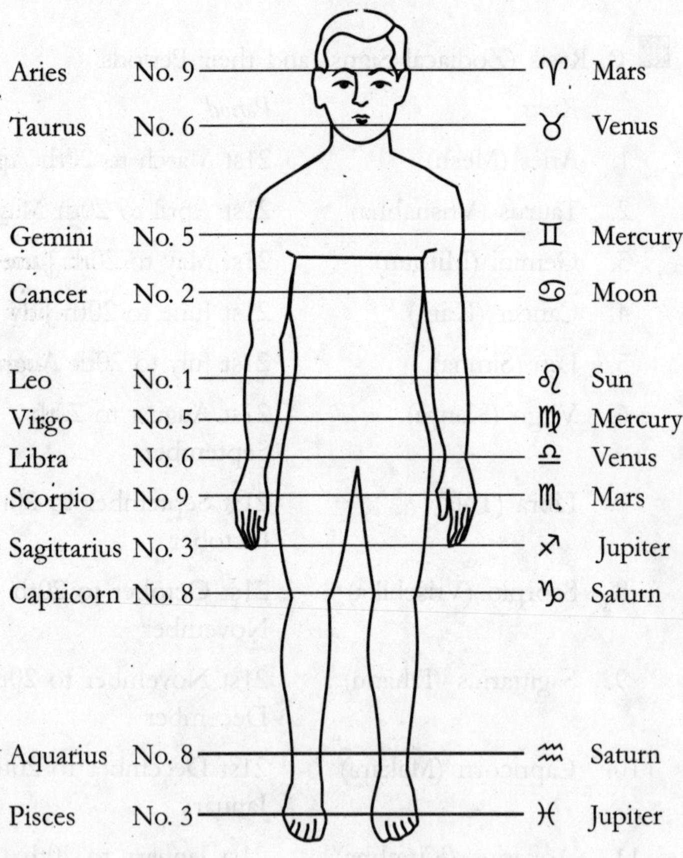

f. How numbers and Rasis (Zodiacs) rule the human body (see figure).

Rasis	*No.*	*Planet*	*Part of the body dominated*
Aries	9	Mars	Head, brain
Taurus	6	Venus	Eyes, ears, nose, tongue, face
Gemini	5	Mercury	Hands, collar-bones, neck, respiratory tract
Caner	2	Moon	Heart, Lungs, Chest, Blood
Leo	1	Sun	Heart, Upper abdomen
Virgo	5	Mercury	Navel, Bones, Lower abdomen
Libra	6	Venus	Groins, Semen, Genitals
Scorpio	9	Mars	Kidney, bladder
Sagittarius	3	Jupiter	Thighs and limbs
Capricorn	8	Saturn	Knees, bones and flesh
Aquarius	8	Saturn	Shanks and breathing
Pisces	3	Jupiter	Feet

For numbers 4 and 7 there are no separate Rasis but only the planets Uranus and Neptune are allotted to them.

g. Division of the Rasis into four Elements

There are four elements, fire, earth, air and water. These elements (Tatvas) indicate their characteristics and the 12 Rasis are divided into these four elements. A person born under a particular Rasi is representative of the element and has his basic qualities according to the element. The elements also show the dangers the person is likely to undergo. For instance, a person governed by the element of fire, should be careful about electricity, stove, burning gas, heat etc. A person with the Earth element has to be careful about snakes, horses and other animals, and also about accidents with vehicles. A person with the Air element runs the danger of falling down from great heights or in air travels and finally a person governed by the water element should be careful while swimming or crossing a river.

A person born under the following periods is governed by the respective elements:

a. *Fire:* 21st March to 20th April; 21st July to 20th August; 21st November to 20th December.

b. *Earth:* 21st April to 20th May; 21st August to 20th September; 21st December to 20th January.

c. *Air:* 21st May to 20th June; 21st September to 20th October; 21st January to 20th February.

d. *Water:* 21st June to 20th July; 21st October to 20th November; 21st February to 20th March.

CHAPTER 3

THE MEANING OF NUMBERS 1 TO 9

The Ruling Number and the Fadic Number

The moment you are born, you are governed by certain numbers. The numbers start dominating all your life. You may not recognise them but they will never escape you. According to the theory of numerology, you are identified only by name and a number.

Every year, as you grow older, numbers will be woven and interwoven in the fabric of your life. You will get opportunities or difficulties in life according to the influence of your number on your life. You will start your schooling and gain a place in your class according to the number you represent. You will complete your education and start your career as per the influence of your number on you. You will occupy your house with a particular number, you get your car or your telephone which has a typical number which governs you. Thus your life unfolds, from the cradle to the grave, according to the influence of numbers on you.

A number is the name of a hidden law. It enters as a vital element. In this book all the cycles and letters are fully explained. Thus you will have all the meanings and implications of the effects of numbers predigested and expressed in a simple way for your guidance. For your intellectual curiosity, the nature of each number is given below:

Number 1: Its nature is intellectual and masculine. It

denotes change and pioneering work. New events, new conditions and travel are indicated when the number 1 appears in the birth-date or a name. It indicates will power to achieve one's goal. However, if the number is not achieved for its goal, it becomes domineering, ruthless, selfish and makes self-gratification its new aim, rationalising its acts as duty.

The planetary equivalent of the number 1 is the Sun, symbolic of life-giving days, creation, vitality, new beginnings, intellectual qualities, inventiveness, genius, originality and brilliance.

Number 2: It symbolises building into form. It is the second deliberate act (after creation). It is feminine in nature and so represents a woman. It is emotional and intuitive. It represents the law of cooperation. It is slow in nature and warm in temperament. If this number appears in a name, it stands for the ability to develop tact and diplomacy. The other side of this number shows timidity, deceit and secrecy. The planetary equivalent of the number 2 is the Moon, symbolic of woman, domesticity, helpfulness, cycles, instability and deliberation.

Number 3: It represents the law of love and affection. It deals with people and reigns over family life and social contacts. This is the number of expression, it brings both the intellect and the intuition to play in the various fields of art. It is a joyful number giving the opportunity for play and entertainment. It is both hopeful and wishful in temperament. If this number appears in a name, it denotes popularity, child, marriage and intrigue. When this number is used for ethical ends, it spells achievement; when it is not, it denotes carelessness, a happy-go-lucky attitude and the scattering of one's talents.

The planetary equivalent of the number 3 is Jupiter, symbolic of good fortune, success, fame, material comfort and happiness.

Number 4: This number shows hard work. It indicates the building of a firm foundation. It endows the power to organise and to work in organisation. It is cold, intellectual and slow in its nature. In a name, it represents discipline; in a cycle, it represents restriction brought about by the need to work hard. It represents the law of justice without mercy, tolerance or sympathy.

The planet allotted to number 4 is Uranus which shows activity, energy, upheavals in life.

Number 5: It stands for law, and for new experiences. It shows change, travel, new friends and it is detached from everything. It means art, interest in religion and in religious institutions. It is rapid in nature, careless in action and speculative in temperament. Above all, it demands freedom of action. This number represents salesmanship and research; it seeks present happiness and cares little for cost or consequence.

The planet of the number 5 is Mercury which is symbolic of speed, communications, changeability, temperament, writing, talking, travel, contacts and radio.

Number 6: It shows the law of material supply. It brings money to those who work hard. It is concerned with education and married life. Harmony at home and in community results from its vibrations. It deals with large groups and institutions. Its aim is to establish beauty, harmony and rhythm. If the number 6 appears in a name, it needs to take responsibility in daily life. It is a combination of the intellectual and the emotional.

The planet of number 6 is Venus. It represents beauty, art, decoration, sympathy and cooperation.

Number 7: This number symbolises the law of culture. It is cold and intellectual in nature. It is the number of inventors, musicians and composers. It deals with the home and the responsibilities of the household. It shows good health and conduct and philosophical nature. When this number is not used properly, it shows deceit and stubbornness.

The planetary equivalent of the number 7 is Neptune. It shows study, research, loneliness, aloofness and mysticism.

Number 8: This number is cold and masculine in nature. It shows good health, energy and endurance. It symbolises justice with mercy. It is the number of power. If this number is lucky, it brings wealth. It shows discipline, method, regularity, system. The power it endows is to be used for the improvement of mankind and if it is diverted to other uses, it brings destruction, in the end destroying itself.

The planet concerned with number 8 is Saturn which deals with the law of Karma. It deals with the occult, with philosophy and with cultural development. It governs the fine arts which do not come under the rule of number 8. This is the number which puts one through life's tests. It establishes the balance of material, spiritual and bodily things.

Number 9: This number is hot and masculine in nature. It shows enthusiasm, activity, energy, quarrels, war, fight and aggression. It is a spiritual number and a person dominated by this number has vibrational force radiating healing powers.

The planet concerned with this number is Mars which is the symbol of war, hot temper, arrogance and strength.

The Rulling Number and the Fadic Number

There are two types of numbers in a birth-date which play an important role in your life. As an example, we take a birth-date, 16-2-1948.

THE RULLING NUMBER:

In the above birth-date, 16 is the date of the month. We have to reduce this date to a single digit, 1 + 6 = 7. This number 7 is the ruling number of the person. It is also considered as a lucky number. All the dates of the month where the final digit comes to 7, such as 16 and 25 are lucky dates and the person should take all his important action on these dates. Supposing he wants to ask for a favour of his superiors, he should select one of these dates for the purpose. If he wants to write an important letter, he should put this date on the letter.

Similarly, all the years in life where the final total after reducing it to a simgle digit is 7 are the important years for that person and usually auspicious events take place in these years. In the present case, the years 7, 16, 25, 34, 43, 52, 61 etc. are significant years. In order to arrive at the same single digit we have to go on adding the number 9 to the earlier figure.

If the date of birth is 12, the ruling number is 3 (1 + 2 = 3). You go on adding 9 to the number 3 and you arrive at the same single digit. Such as 3 + 9 = 12 (i.e. 3). 12 + 9 = 21 (i.e. 3). 21 + 9 = 30 (i.e. 3) etc. All these dates 3, 12, 21, 30 are lucky dates and all the years in life making up 3 are lucky years. At these years of his life, he may get through his examination, he may complete his educational career, or he may get his first job, or he may get a promotion or he may be married, or he may book a new flat for his residence, or he may get a child, or may get property by inheritance, and so on and so forth.

THE FADIC NUMBER:

This is also called the 'Fate Number' or the 'Number of Destiny'. In this case a total of all the numbers in a birth-date is to be taken. In the above illustration, the complete birth date is 16-2-1948. We have to add all the digits in the birth date, thus:

1 + 6 + 2 + 1 + 9 + 4 + 8 = 31.

Add 3 + 1 = 4. This 4 is called the Fadic Number. The significance of this number is that it goes on repeating and recurring in the life of the person whether he or she desires it or not. The events that take place may be either good or bad but they are important and significant events and the person has no control over the number and the events. Suppose it is failure in college or the winning of a gold medal, the date on which either of these events take place will be governed by the number 4 in which case either the total of all the numbers of that particular date will be 4 or the date of the month when the incident took place will be 4.

After explaining how to find out our lucky number and the fadic number, I shall proceed further with the individual numbers from 1 to 9 and describe them from various angles.

CHAPTER 4

NUMBER 1

All those born on the 1st, 10th, 19th or 28th of any month are governed by number 1 and this is their ruling number.

Character

BORN ON THE 1st OF THE MONTH:

This number is governed by the planet Sun and shows originality, activity, energy, enthusiasm, art and brilliance. If you are born on any of the above dates, you are spontaneous, respond to nature and have the capacity to enjoy life. The planet Sun gives intellectual capacity and therefore you are attracted to pursuits and work of a mental rather than of a physical character and are associated with learning, education and the teaching or training of others. You have the capacity to hold executive and administrative positions. Your personality is independent but also has adaptability to some extent. You gain knowledge through observation and travel. You have an ability for writing certain forms of literary work, journalism and have contact with newspapers and associated publications.

You have an active and highly creative turn of mind. To follow or obey orders is distasteful to you. Since you are self-reliant, and confident of your abilities, you never hesitate to tackle the most difficult or the most abstruse of problems. Courage, initiative and leadership distinguish you.

You are an artist and have many talents in you but they are

all spontaneous. You have a taste for everything but choose only the beautiful. You are gifted with intuition and hardly go deep into any subject. Even then you can influence others with your knowledge and flash. These characteristics makes you a hero of the drawing room. You are changeable and not constant in your friendship. You are honest and acknowledge your faults. You have a quick grasp of any subject and can participate spontaneously in conversation. You have a religious attitude but not in a fanatic or superstitious way. You also learn the occult sciences and do wonders with your natural gift of intuition. By nature, you are cheerful, happy and bright and your outlook on life is very optimistic. You are independent in thought and action and have strong will-power. Sometimes you are obstinate and selfish. You are fond of inventions and have creative talents. You are a better judge of human nature than the average individual. A new idea is a greater thrill to you than money in the bank. You will always remain young because of your love of new ideas. It is better that you learn to work well with others so that you can benefit in life as well as improve the impression that you make.

BORN ON THE 10TH OF THE MONTH:

You have all the basic characteristics as explained for number 1, so first read those characteristics and then read your own as born on the 10th.

All forms of change, conversion and transmutation are your fields of activity. You supply the mental power, agility and energy to take the river and make it a dynamo. You are the executive in your personality and can lead to victory where others fear to tread. You have creative originality and you enjoy tackling a good hard problem. You are impressive with a magnetic personality and are respected for your knowledge and intelligence. You obtain financial benefits from relatives such as father, father-in-law, wife, mother, etc. You will get success after your 46th year. You get good position in service and succeed in business also. You have broad shoulders and manly figure.

Whilst there is an undoubted brilliance of thought and inspiration and a capacity to take quick and constructive decisions, you find difficulty in exercising adaptability to such conditions and hence you take impulsive and unwise decisions regarding changes and in connection with prevailing associations. Your erratic tendencies result in sudden upsets and disputes and you will have disturbance in your working or business interests and you run the risk of losing a job or a position. You like to take the law in your own hands, and will go your own way irrespective of the desires or commands of others. In fact, any attempt on the part of people to force you to follow their way will only make you go in the opposite direction. You should take care not to become overbearing, for the prestige you now command might suffer if you did.

You can get fame or notoriety depending upon your will-power and character. Usually you have good health and quickly recover from sickness. You like to help others but hardly get any response from them. This is particularly so in the case of relatives.

BORN ON THE 19TH OF THE MONTH:

You have all the basic characteristics as explained for number 1 above, so first go through them and then read your own as stated below:

You are very active, energetic and enthusiastic. You have an aptitude for research and like to handle subjects in systematic and methodical ways. You take quick decisions and always like to keep yourself busy in some concrete project or the other. Your main hobby is sports, and you are interested in several games such as horse-riding, shooting, and other athletic games. You are hasty and impetuous in love affairs which end in quarrels. You are courageous and have force of character. You like to help others even when it means going out of your way. You have the ability to maintain the secrets of others and others can confide in you. It is rather difficult for others to understand you. Even when you are in the company of others, you feel lonely at heart. You are obstinate and find it difficult to extend cooperation to others. You are prudent and notice even a trivial thing. You are not an excellent speaker but can explain yourself best in writing. You can therefore be a good writer.

You have experiences of every kind which widen your perceptions and enhance your wisdom. The everlasting emotions of the human race course through your temperament, such as love, hate, and self preservation.

You are very expressive and positive in word, act and feeling. Fortune follows you but as adventure beckons, you are likely to pick up and travel on to other pastures. Your symbol is the overturning wheel from creation to completion and therefore you have varied experiences. You have to learn to let the benefits accrue so that the uncertainties of life never leave you high or dry.

BORN ON THE 28TH OF THE MONTH:

You have all the basic characteristics of the number 1 explained above, so first go through them and then read your own as spelt out below:

You are very generous and spend on charitable works such

as schools, institutions, hospitals, etc. You are not as lucky as number 1, 10 and 19 and have to undergo difficulties in public and private life. You should select your marriage partner very carefully. You have to provide for the future as you are likely to lose through trust in others. You are also likely to make many changes in your career. You hardly ever reveal your emotions and therefore appear cold. You have an unyielding will-power and do not hesitate to carry out your plans. So it is better for you to work with a collaboration or partner than go it alone.

Do not be too independent in your thoughts or actions. If you are considered completely self-sufficient, you may lose the warmth of the friendships you now posses.

Finance

You are a lucky person as far as your financial status is concerned. Even though you are extravagant due to your over enthusiastic personality, you also earn enough to maintain your ostentatious disposition in life. You may not amass wealth but your personality and behaviour will make others believe that you are a rich person. You have temptations for gambling and if not controlled in time, you may lose to a great extent. For your lucky money number, please refer to Chapter 15.

Vocation

The main difficulty with you is your attitude not to stick to any one profession or job for a long time. Usually, every three years there is a change in your carrier. You are however, suitable for advertising concerns, the newspaper business, the cinema industry and can also be successful in theatrical performances. You can show your art as an interior decorator./ Since you are a good sales-man, you should choose vocation which involves relations with foreign commodities. You are a leader and can be the head of a department, a managing director, etc. You can succeed as a surgeon, a jeweller, or electrician, or in projects, involving research.

Health

On the whole you are a happy-go-lucky fellow and normally of good health. You will enjoy good health so long as you do not give way to mental strain or worry. Otherwise there will be a reaction on the nerves with a liability to nervous disorders and should mental tension be permitted to go to an extreme, to nervous breakdowns. On the other hand maintaining of a cheerful and optimistic outlook on life, which you have undoubtedly the capacity to maintain, will enable you to keep in good health and to enjoy many of the social and pleasurable amenities of life and to do a considerable amount of travel.

Marriage And Friends

You have a natural attraction towards persons born in the period between 21st July and 20th August, between 21st November and 20th December and between 21st March and 20th April. It is therefore advisable that you select your marriage partner from this period. You also have an affinity for those who are governed by numbers 1, 4, 5, 7 and their corresponding multiples. You will be attracted towards intellectual types and yet because of the intellectual bias, there can be an absence of passion and warmth which, despite your own intellectual conception of affairs, you will desire. Hence it will be somewhat difficult to bring about desired developments. The marriage partner can be contacted whilst on a journey or as a result of attending a lecture or a discussion group.

NUMBER 1 AS HUSBAND:

You are generous and desire your wife to shine in society. You want your family member to dance to your tune, and you will not tolerate disrespect. You have a kind and loving disposition and a loving heart.

NUMBER 1 AS WIFE:

You are aristocratic by temperament and attract people to your home and command great respect. You need a virile husband who can offer the romantic outlets that your passionate nature requires.

As a number 1 person are always predisposed to marriage and you are fond of your helpmate provided he is also of equal enthusiasm and has a love of beauty and of dress, at home and in public. It is however, often seen that you hardly get a companion of your choice, with the result that you are often disappointed in your married life.

Friends

Your best friends are those who are governed by numbers 1, 3, 4, 5, 7 and 9.

Fortunate Days

Your lucky days are Sundays, Mondays and Thursdays.

Lucky Colors

You should use all shades of gold and yellow and also of orange and purple as your lucky colours.

Lucky Jewels and Stones

Your lucky jewels are ruby and emerald and lucky stones are moonstone and pale green stone.

Important Years

Your important years in life are: 1, 19, 28, 37, 46, 55, 64, 73 etc. Mostly good and auspicious events take place during these years. You will either get your first graduation or first job or your promotion or a house or your marriage or any other events which we can say is auspicious.

Your good qualities and drawbacks are as under:

Good Qualities	*Drawbacks*
Aspiration	Aloofness
Attack	Domination
Authority	Impertinence
Confidence	Inflexibility
Determination	Pride
Research	Show
Vigour	Spendthrift

Important:

Please also refer to the month you are born in. Combine your characteristics, lucky days, colours and jewels shown by your number and also by the month you are born in and then find out the common factors and arrive at the final conclusion.

The study of numbers is nothing but the study of psychoanalysis. The deep-rooted feelings, sentiments, emotions, ambitions and abilities are best represented by numbers. You can take advantage of your abilities and try to come over your drawbacks so that life will be easy and successful.

However, if you do not find any common factor, then follow the lucky days, colours and the jewels as shown by your Ruling Number and not by the month.

Fadic Number 1

Fadic number is the single number arrived at after totalling all the numbers in your complete birth-date. If the total of your complete birth date is 1, it shows the following:

Your long range ambition will be realised. Others will seek your advice and will look to you for leadership. The work you take in hand will ultimately achieve prosperity. However, you may also face trouble because of your arrogance. You may hurt your friends due to lack of sheer consideration on your part.

Financially you may benefit and there may be a good rise in your income. It will be necessary for you to take sufficient rest, which is of course very difficult for you, otherwise it may work on your nerves.

If your Fadic number is 1, your speech is direct, forceful and candid. Your special characteristic is your love for advice-giving, albeit with the highest motives.

Important Note

In order to get full benefit of the things explained herein and to achieve success in life you should act upon the following recommendations:

1. You should do all your important work on your lucky days and dates. You may try your luck in lottery by purchasing a ticket where the total of all numbers works out to your lucky number or where the last digit is your lucky number.
2. You can gain confidence if you make use of your lucky colours for painting your living room or bed room, or use these colours while selecting your clothes.

3. You can increase the vibrations of your personality by wearing your lucky jewels.
4. You can plan all your important activities during your important years.

CHAPTER 5

NUMBER 2

All those born on 2nd, 11th, 20th or 29th of any month are governed by number 2 and this is their ruling number.

Character

BORN ON THE 2ND OF THE MONTH:

This number is governed by the planet Moon. It shows high imagination, idealism and a dreamy nature. You are the executor of the plans and projects instituted or organised by others. This does not mean that you lack originality but that your originality lies in the direction of making ways and means to carry out a blue print or design made by someone else. You are considerate, unselfish and always thoughtful of the feelings and wishes of others. You are a good partner and a collaborator. You have a natural power of discrimination and perception which will express itself through business and associated channels. You will be able to carry out the details of affairs without losing sight of the ultimate goal towards which you are working. You love neatness and tidiness and prefer proper discipline to lackadaisical methods.

You have fantasies and lack a practical approach. Many times you revel in your own dreams and therefore shun society. You do not enjoy the company of others as you find them too ordinary for your imaginary world. You love natural and beautiful things in life such as the sea, flowers, scenery and the vastness of the sky. You take pleasure in spending hours in the company of the high tides of the sea or in reverting your eyes to the galaxy of the stars in the sky.

You are very unsteady, fickle-minded and a lover of change. You therefore have a fancy for travel, especially long travels which satisfy your urge for the life of the imagination.

It is better to avoid letting others take advantage of your good nature.

BORN ON THE 11TH OF THE MONTH:

You have all the basic characteristics explained for number 2, so first read those characteristics and then read your own as born on the 11th of the month.

This date is considered as a master power number. You have high intuition and you are inspired by high ideals. Electric power almost vibrates from your personal magnetism and you are generally the master of every situation. Executive ability is prominent in your make-up and your mind is creative, original and alert. You seek to shield those you love and you like the role of the provider. You are modest and do not like to show off your abilities and talents. The subtler things in life appeal to you. You like detective stories as will as mystic philosophy. You have a great magnetism for people but you are not too quick to part with your affections. You can influence people by your mental and verbal; suggestions and in so doing will get them to react and do things that are in accord with your own desires. You have much latent psychic ability which you can express as a result of proper development, for the planet Moon gives you a capacity for clairvoyance, sometimes for trance, mediumship and also for psychometry. You should learn to relax with the lighter pleasures of the mind and spirit. Too much concentration inclines you to depression which you must try to avoid.

You are usually successful in life and in love and get honour, position and authority. You are loyal to your friends and are of royal disposition. You should guard yourself from secret enemies.

BORN ON THE 20TH OF THE MONTH:

You have all the basic characteristics explained for number 2 above, so first read those characteristic and then read your own as born on the 20th of the month.

You have many friends and benefit through wealthy women. You have a flair for writing and can make a name as an author or a novelist. Your prosperity lies near water, i.e. a river or the sea. This birth-date shows new plans, and new resolutions for the betterment of people at large. If this date comes in connection with the future events, it shows delays. You are warm hearted, affectionate and answer every call for help.

BORN ON THE 29TH OF THE MONTH:

You have all the basic qualities that are explained for the number 2; so you should first go through them and then read your own as born on the 29th of the month.

You have the ability to attract people towards you. You are cooperative but in an intellectual way rather than a warm-hearted way. You have instinct to understand people and your wide perception makes you a citizen of the world. You take a deep interest in your home life, and always see to it that your family is provided for with all necessities.

However, you are very moody and changing and, therefore, uncertain about your action. You are courageous and bold but take risks in life and do not stick to anything till the end. You are intelligent and also a deep thinker but there is a tendency in you to carry everything to extremes.

Finance

You do not like to do any hard work and therefore, your constitution as such is lethargic. You also do not have the physical capacity to stand the strain of everyday life. The outcome, therefore, is your mediocre financial status. You can improve your financial conditions provided you create art out of your imagination.

In order to be successful in financial matters, please refer to Chapter 15 to find out your lucky money number and start all your financial activities on that number.

Vocation

There are innumerable vocations these days, and it is not possible to pinpoint any one as such. However the vocations given below indicate the utility of your inherent abilities which can lead you to a successful life.

The high imaginative power that you possess will make you successful as a good composer of music or a writer of fiction or romance stories. You can equally be a good artist and create works of everlasting value. You have a great vocabulary and linguistic capacities among all other number which can make you a good teacher or a professor of various languages. The planet Moon is concerned with liquids and so you have every opportunity to be a good chemist or an analyst or you can be successful in the chemical industry or even as a dentist or a surgeon.

Health

You have to take care of your digestive system and your bowels. Some trouble towards suffering from various forms of colic, infection of intestinal digestion, neuralgia of the intestine, diarrhoea, constipation, typhoid and enteric fever is denoted. Any sluggishness of the digestive organs should be promptly remedied as otherwise the accumulation of waste matter in the system can be the originating cause of other ailments of a more serious character.

Another factor affecting your health is the poor blood circulation resulting in anaemia and a weak heart. Since the Moon is your ruling planet, the uneasiness which is a prominent characteristic, creates mental worries and sleeplessness. You are also susceptible to diabetes and asthmatic trouble.

Marriage And Friends

You have a natural attraction towards person born in the period between 21st October and 20th November and between 19th February and 20th March. It is, therefore, advisable that you select your marriage partner from this period. You also have an affinity for those who are governed by numbers 2.. 4 and 6. In this case, please also refer to the month you are born in and see your inclination and find out the common factor. If there is no common factor, then go by the recommendation given above.

The best type of partner is shown to be someone who is intellectual but who can also give thought to what may be termed 'creature comforts' and who will be practical so far as financial and kindred matters are concerned. You will use quite a deal of discrimination in matters to do with the affectional and marital side of life.

NUMBER 2 AS HUSBAND:

You have a natural love and attraction for home more perhaps than any other type. There are two types of husbands belonging to this number; one is dominating and exacting. He is fault-finding and nothing satisfies him. The other type is passive, lazy and indulgent. He will marry for the sake of money so that he may ultimately live in comfort.

NUMBER 2 AS WIFE:

As a wife, you are sympathetic, affectionate and devoted. You are satisfied with anything your husband provides you. However you are moody, changeable and sensitive. You will not disturb your husband but do the things in your own way. Though you will carry out your responsibilities as a housewife, you are not much interested in spending your time in the kitchen.

As a number 2 person, you are somewhat cold and do not have the fire of passion. Sometimes you may select a partner who is either far older or younger than yourself.

Friends

Your best friends are those who are governed by numbers 2, 4, 6 and 9.

Fortunate Days

Your lucky days are Mondays, Tuesdays and Fridays.

Lucky Colours

You should always use all shades of white, cream or blue as these are your lucky colours.

Lucky Jewels And Stones

Your lucky jewels are pearls and diamonds and lucky stones are moonstone and agate.

Important Years In Life

Your important years in life are 2, 11, 20, 29, 38, 47, 56, 65, 74 etc. where the final single digit comes to 2. Mostly good and auspicious events take place during these years. You will either get your graduation or your job or your promotion or a house or your marriage or any other event which we can say is auspicious.

Your good qualities and drawbacks are as under:

Good Qualities	*Drawbacks*
Sympathy	Coldness
Fellowship	Envy
Honesty	Haste
Imagination	Intervention
Simplicity	Shyness
Ideality	Whimsicality

Important:

Please also refer to the month you are born in. Combine your characteristics, lucky days, colours and jewels shown by your number and also by the month you are born in and then find out the common factors and arrive at the final conclusion.

However, if you do not find any common factor, then follow the lucky days, colours and the jewels as shown by your Ruling Number and not by the month.

The study of numbers is nothing but the study of psycho-analysis. The deep-rooted feelings, sentiments, emotions, ambitions and abilities are best represented by numbers. You can take advantage of your abilities and try to come over your drawbacks so that life will be easy and successful.

Fadic Number 2

Fadic number is the single number arrived at after totalling all the numbers in your complete birth-date. If the total of your complete birth-date is 2, it shows the following:

You dislike quarrels and will go to great length to avoid them. You will attempt a compromise every time rather than force the issue. You like to work quietly and prefer to remain in the background without boasting or advertising yourself. Young people and children will always play an important role in your life. You are extremely sensitive to the external environment. Your financial prospects improve by work which will bring you into direct touch with the public. You will benefit more from work done for others than when working on your own account.

Important Note

In order to get full benefit of the things explained herein and to achieve success in life you should act upon the following recommendations:

1. You should do all your important work on your lucky days and dates. You may try your luck in lottery by purchasing a ticket where the total of all numbers works out to your lucky number or where the last digit is your lucky number.
2. You can gain confidence if you make use of your lucky colours for painting your living room or bed room, or use these colours while selecting your clothes.
3. You can increase the vibrations of your personality by wearing your lucky jewels.
4. You can plan all your important activities during your important years.

CHAPTER 6

NUMBER 3

All those born on 3rd, 12th, 21st or 30th of any month are governed by number 3 and this is their ruling number.

Character

BORN ON THE 3RD OF THE MONTH:

This number is governed by the planet Jupiter. It stands for morality, pure love and justice with mercy and is known as the greatest benefic and the uplifter. The vibrations emitted by this number are essentially harmonious and they lead to sympathy and untiring effort to do good to all, devout piety and true dignity. The abuse of the same vibrations causes the stimulation of Jupiterian virtues leading to hypocrisy, especially in religious matters. Good nature is marred by excess in many directions.

You are usually lucky in life. Vibrations radiating through you attract all that is good to you and your affairs prosper as a consequence. Judges who give wise decisions and merciful sentences, physicians and church dignitaries, the world's teachers and philosophers are all mostly governed by the number 3. Since your birth-date is significant of dealings with the masses and of being in the public eye in some capacity, popularity and contact with large numbers of people occupy your time to a large extent. Cleverness and natural charm bring a lot of friends to you and you are the centre of every group's attention. You are versatile, to the extent of sometimes being puzzled as to what form of expression your talents should take. You are for this reason somewhat inclined to scatter your talents and should learn that specialization in a single field of your choice will bring greater rewards than dabbling in many.

You have a strong desire for peace and harmony and become sensitive to anything of a deliberately discordant nature. You are naturally courteous and desirous of being on good terms with other people, but you will always need to maintain a proper independent spirit so as to prevent certain people from imposing upon you, as they are aware of your natural disinclination to enter into arguments or disputes. You can be adaptable but you can also be very easily upset by adverse criticism or temporary rebuffs and inclined to take things more to heart than you should do.

You are confident about your ability. You are self-reliant and take your own decisions. You have a habit of talking loudly. You like to observe form, order and law. Your passions are healthy, spontaneous and without inhibitions. You are free in your expression.

You take an active interest in sports and outdoor activities from your earliest youth. You have tremendous enthusiasm and are not self-centered. Your intellect is of a very high quality. You have a kind of vision that understands the world and love it for what it is, and not for what it ought to be. You are tolerant, humorous and truthful. You have a broad mind and entirely lack malice or petty jealousies.

Your main characteristics are ambition, leadership, religion, pride, honour, love for nature, enthusiasm, generosity, respect and reverence.

BORN ON THE 12TH OF THE MONTH:

You have all the basic characteristics explained for number 3 above, so first read them and then read your own as born on the 12th of the month.

You are rather sensitive and there will be extremes of temperament and ability. Sometimes you will be extremely cheerful and optimistic. When you express this side of your nature, together with a degree of sympathy and understanding for others who are in trouble or difficulty, you will create considerable popularity and will make a great deal of progress. On the other hand, you can give way to extreme sensitiveness and allow yourself to feel hurt at the careless or thoughtless speech or action of others and will try to cover this up by expressing an apparent air of indifference which will be rather puzzling to those around you, as they will not be aware of having done anything to warrant being ignored by you.

As born on the 12th of the month, you are a well-balanced person, highly endowed in attractive physical and mental traits. In all things, you exercise good judgement and your actions are motivated by the highest moral and ethical standards. Social life holds a great attraction for you and you set the pace and create the fads.

Authority and honors are the significant aspects of your life. You have vanity and are proud, ambitious and aspiring. You are fond of pleasures and are attracted to the opposite sex. You like to sacrifice for others but become instead a victim of others' plans and intrigues. You are quick to notice trifles. You have lofty ideals and your relations with others are smooth and harmonious.

BORN ON THE 21ST OF THE MONTH:

You have all the basic characteristics as explained for the

number 3, therefore first go through those characteristics and then read your own which are as under.

You are kind, generous and loving. You achieve fame, reputation and honour at a very late age. You are cheerful and fond of travel. You have a strong feeling of self respect. Surprisingly, you have a suspicious nature.

You are considered lucky because you have good fortune, an interesting personality and a magnetic way about you. The lighter and glittering side of life appeals to you and you are the centre of the social circle. You like many people and you are popular with both sexes. You will always have the desire to exercise authority and a degree of domination over others.

BORN ON THE 30TH OF THE MONTH:

You have all the basic characteristics explained for number 3 above, so first read them and then read your own as born on 30th of the month.

You have a strong power of attraction and, therefore, friends always gather round you. You like social life but this does not mean that there is no serious side to your nature. In fact, you like to fulfil every duty of your career. You have great potentialities but do not fritter away your talents or money where they will go to waste. You are fortunate, generous and optimistic. You have a noble and religious mind. You like to travel and visit places of pilgrimage. You can be successful as a teacher, or as an educationist or in administration. You appear gentle and sincere but have a hidden characteristic. You may be active but you are restless. When you are face to face with difficulties, you are strong enough to overcome them.

Finance

You are lucky in financial matters and somehow manage to get enough for your requirement. You also get opportunities for high grade positions in life and thereby earn quite a lot. Your ambition, leadership and enthusiasm always push you forward and usually you get all the comforts in life. You are always early out of puberty and poverty.

In order to be successful in financial matters, please refer to Chapter 15 and find out your lucky money number and start all your financial activities on that number.

Vocation

Now-a-days, there are innumerable vocations and it is not possible to pin-point any one as such. However, the vocations given below indicate the utility of your inherent abilities which, if brought into practice, will lead you to be a successful personality in life.

Your love for position and command makes you a politician. I have observed certain persons of this number occupying very high posts such as ministers, ambassadors, judges and secretaries. You are cut out for public life, statesmanship, high offices etc., it may be in the army or in the church. You are a good teacher as well as a preacher. Professions of doctors, bankers, advertiser and actors are also suitable for you.

Health

On the whole you will have good health and also the power of speedy recuperation. Even then, you are susceptible to certain sicknesses. The number 3 has a major influence on the blood and the arterial system. It also governs the sense of smell, the lumber region, the skin and the kidneys. You are, therefore, liable to suffer from chest and lung disorders, throat afflictions, gout and sudden fevers. You should try to avoid excess of sugar in the system. Any tendency towards diabetes should receive immediate attention.

Marriage And Friends

You have a natural attraction towards those born in the period from 21st June to 20th July and from 21st October to 20th November. It is, therefore, advisable that you find your marriage partner from this period. You also have affinity for those who are governed by numbers 3, 6, 7 and 9. Therefore, select your partner from the series of these numbers and from the above period.

NUMBER 3 AS HUSBAND:

As a general rule, you attain puberty at an early age and marry early. However, as you are ambitious, your ambitions also make you expect too many things from your wife and thus you become disappointed. You desire to have a wife of whom you would be proud. She should have an attractive personality, a commanding presence, charming manners and intelligence. It will be good for you to choose a number 3 person or a number 6 person as your life partner. You are most loving, thoughtful and considerate. Your passions are adventurous and demand immediate satisfaction.

NUMBER 3 AS WIFE:

You are a good companion to your husband. You are not an intruder but take an active interest in the business of your husband. You are efficient in house-keeping and have a sympathetic and balanced outlook on your children. Your passions are healthy and joyous and your approach to physical love is highly refined and inspiring.

Friends

Your best friends are those governed by numbers 1, 3, 5, 6 and 7.

Fortunate Days

Your lucky days are Tuesdays, Thursdays and Fridays.

Lucky Colours

You should use all shades of yellow, violet, purple and green as these are your lucky colours.

Lucky Jewels And Stones

Your lucky jewel is topaz, and your lucky stones are amethyst and cat's eye.

Important Years In Life

Your important years are 3, 12, 21, 30, 39, 48, 57, 66 and 75 etc. Mostly good and auspicious events take place during these years. You will either get your graduation, or first job, or your promotion, or a house or your marriage, or any other event which we can call auspicious.

Your good qualities and drawbacks are as under:

Qualities	*Drawbacks*
Ambition	Cruelty
Dignity	Dictatorship
Individuality	Hypocrisy
Philosophy	Spendthrift
Prestige	Vanity

Important:

Please also refer to the month you are born in. Combine

your characteristics, lucky days, colours and jewels shown by your number and also by the month you are born in and then find out the common factors and arrive at the final conclusion.

However, if you do not find any common factor, then follow the lucky days, colours and the jewels as shown by your Ruling Number and not by the month.

The study of numbers is nothing but the study of psycho-analysis. The deep-rooted feelings, sentiments, emotions, ambitions and abilities are best represented by numbers. You can take advantage of your abilities and try to come over your drawbacks so that life will be easy and successful.

Fadic Number 3

Fadic number is the single number arrived at after totalling all the numbers in your complete birth-date. If the total of your complete birth date is 3, it shows the following:

Money questions will always be of exceptional significance. Opportunities to gain or lose substantially will be constantly coming their way but with average common sense it would be possible to secure a considerable improvement in your financial status.

Many of your friends will be formed in connection with your career. Generally you will find yourself among successful people.

On the whole you will have good health but you should take care about troubles connected with the digestion

Important Note

In order to get full benefit of the things explained herein and to achieve success in life you should act upon the following recommendations:

1. You should do all your important work on your lucky days and dates. You may try your luck in lottery by purchasing a ticket where the total of all numbers works out to your lucky number or where the last digit is your lucky number.
2. You can gain confidence if you make use of your lucky colours for painting your living room or bed room, or use these colours while selecting your clothes.
3. You can increase the vibrations of your personality by wearing your lucky jewels.
4. You can plan all your important activities during your important years.

CHAPTER 7

NUMBER 4

All those born on 4th, 13th, 22nd or 31st of any month are governed by number 4 and this is their ruling number.

Character

BORN ON THE 4TH OF THE MONTH:

This number is governed by the planet Uranus and shows energy, force and advancement. It shows revolution and unexpected happenings in life. Usually, the changes that take place are for the better. This number represents the higher faculties of the mind. It shows activity and intelligence engaged in the reconstruction or the betterment of human life. The peculiar nature of this number is that it constantly aims at changes in life and society and is after the liberation of the mind from the bondage of environment and society. It dislikes hypocrisy and loves art and music.

In general, you have the same characteristics as that of number 1, but these characteristics are in a dormant condition. It means you are required to be pushed forward so that you can show your abilities. Your nature is to oppose the views of others or to advance arguments with the result that you are often misunderstood and make a great number of secret enemies who constantly work against you.

You are reserved and sometimes secretive. You will display considerable resourcefulness in the handling of people and will work through difficulties more easily than may be anticipated. You will express more resistance and fighting capacity than those around you. You have courage and your own convictions to say and do the things you consider to be correct.

Your life is an active and creative one. You are always busy with work that will advance the world, and promote goodwill among men. You are reliable and trustworthy and earn a good reputation in life.

BORN ON THE 13TH OF THE MONTH:

You have all the basic characteristics explained for number 4 above, so first read them and then read your own as born on the 13th of the month.

You have leadership and you enjoy your role. The keynote of your thinking and actions is structure. You have an infinite capacity for work which amounts to the classical definition of genius. You are satisfied when others enjoy your company. You like to formulate and plan very carefully. Precision and efficiency mark your efforts, and success crowns them. You like to move in intellectual circles.

You are independent, self-willed, active and desirous of being in command of affairs. You are courageous by nature and not likely to be afraid of facing danger when it arises. It is better you control your aggressive impulse and undue independence. You always like to fight against conditions of an unfair and restrictive nature. Your success and career start after your 31st year.

BORN ON THE 22ND OF THE MONTH:

You have all the basic characteristics explained for number 4 above, so first read them and then read your own as born on 22nd of the month.

This date shows the season of the year when you were born and will have a determining influence over your character. You have an organising ability and the capacity to hold the position of authority. You have a degree of pride and dignity and it will be relatively easy to obtain recognition of your abilities. The year from 40 to 60 will bring you to the zenith of your career. Many times you will be lonely because others will not reach up to your standard of thought and comprehension. The first half of life will be hard, but the second half can bring a realisation of earlier ambitions and desires. You may be inclined to be over conservative in carrying out inspirational programmes. Doubts rarely assail you because of your over-confidence. In life you have so much to give and gain, so go and build.

You are tall with good eyes. Usually you occupy good positions but these without much responsibility. You are rather easy going, unsteady in nature. Sometimes your actions are spasmodic. On the whole, you are lucky in your affairs and benefit from the opposite sex. You are happy with your family life but are also fond of a companion. Your social field is limited and you have few friends. You do not care for disputes. You have too much economy of sentiments.

BORN ON THE 31ST OF THE MONTH:

You have all the basic characteristics explained for number 4 above, so first read them and then read your own as born on the 31st of the month.

You have ambition, pride and austerity. You are interested in honourable occupations such as working with charitable institutions, institutions for the deaf and dumb, the physically handicapped etc. You get success after your 40th year but you expect quick results and early reputation. You are lucky in financial matters. You are realistic and of strong will power. You love travelling.

You can be a good social leader even though you like to stick to your routine schedule. You go by your judgement and discrimination. You have creative ideas and know very well how to carry them out with the help of right people.

Finance

As regards finance and monetary status, you are usually well settled in life, though you experience delays and difficulties in your undertakings. You may not amass wealth but can maintain a show of wealth. You are a spendthrift and your home is well decorated. Your financial prosperity usually starts after the age of 40.

In order to be successful in financial matters, please refer to Chapter 15 and find out your lucky money number and start all your financial activities on that number.

Vocation

Nowadays, there are innumerable vocations and it is not possible to pinpoint any one as such. However, the vocations given below indicate the utility of your inherent abilities which, if brought into practice, will lead you to be a successful personality in life. You will be successful in trade such as transport, electricity and all sorts of machinery. You will be equally successful as an engineer, a building contractor, a scientist or an industrialist. You are also attracted towards mystic subjects such as palmistry and astrology and can do well in these subjects.

Health

You will enjoy good health due to your physical strength

and endurance, provided of course that you observe normal habits of life. However, you are also susceptible to certain weaknesses of health and you have to take care of the trouble arising out of bad functioning of the kidney or the bladder. Proper precautions should be taken when you are in the vicinity of people suffering from infections ailments.

In addition to the above weaknesses, your respiratory system is usually weak and you suffer from breathlessness. Your knees, shanks and feet are also affected.

Marriage And Friends

You have a natural attraction towards persons born in the period between 19th February and 20th March and between 21st October and 20th November. It is, therefore, advisable that you select your marriage partner from this period. You also have an affinity for those who are governed by numbers 1, 2, 4, 7 and 8.

NUMBER 4 AS HUSBAND:

You are affectionate and emotional. You expect a partner who has an active temperament and quite a deal of physical courage. You are quite possessive which may create unpleasantness. You are shrewd and intelligent and expect your wife to share your views. You are dominating and want all affairs of the house to run as per your desire. You are generous and have a kind and loving heart.

NUMBER 4 AS WIFE:

You are smart and attractive. You have the art of dressing well and have a strong will power. You aim at several things but hardly succeed in getting mastery over even one. You love interior decoration but do not have the capacity to work hard at it, and you will get it done through others. You are many times dictatorial and moody and spoil your day due to your own whimsical nature. You love your home but are not attached to it very much. You are often uneasy and it is better for you to find a friend governed by number 1 or 2. You are headstrong and sometimes cruel. You always make others dance to your tune. This is more so if you are born during the period of Mars and on the 22nd of a month such as 22nd March, 22nd April, 22nd October, 22nd November and even 22nd December.

Friends

Your best friends are those who are governed by numbers 1, 2, 4, 5, 7, 8 and 9.

Fortunate Days

Your lucky days are Sundays, Mondays and Saturdays.

Lucky Colours

Your lucky colours are electric blue, electric grey, white and maroon.

Lucky Jewels And Stones

Your lucky jewels are diamond, coral and pearl

Important Years In Life

Your important years are 4, 13, 22, 31, 40, 49, 58, 67 and 76 etc. Mostly good and auspicious events take place during these years. You will either get your graduation, or first job or your promotion or a house or your marriage, or any other events which we can call auspicious.

Your good qualities and drawbacks are as under:

Good Qualities	*Drawbacks*
Activity	Changeable
Endurance	Dominating
Energy	Stubborn
Reliability	Vindictive
Method and system	Jealous

Important:

Please also refer to the month you are born in. Combine your characteristics, lucky days, colours and jewels shown by your number and also by the month you are born in and then find out the common factors and arrive at the final conclusion.

However, if you do not find any common factor, then follow the lucky days, colours and the jewels as shown by your Ruling Number and not by the month.

The study of numbers is nothing but the study of psycho-analysis. The deep-rooted feelings, sentiments, emotions, ambitions and abilities are best represented by numbers. You can take advantage of your abilities and try to over come your drawbacks so that life will be easy and successful.

Fadic Number 4

Fadic number is the single number arrived at after totalling all the numbers in your complete birth-date. If the total of your complete birth date is 4, it shows the following:

Throughout life you will face one dilemma after another, but fortunately your attitude will be confident and resourceful. You will enjoy the constant sense of adventure. You will have openings to show great originality, and your many fresh ideas will make good headway. Great independence will be sought and won. It is necessary that you keep your plans fairly elastic because it will be necessary to revise them frequently.

You will have numerous contacts and will come across at least one person of an eccentric nature who is sure to appear a diverting companion. You will enjoy good health provided you do not allow nervous afflictions to go without treatment. Your occupation is likely to be in the technical field, especially engineering and electrical trades.

Important Note

In order to get full benefit of the things explained herein and to achieve success in life you should act upon the following recommendations:

1. You should do all your important work on your lucky days and dates. You may try your luck in lottery by purchasing a ticket where the total of all numbers works out to your lucky number or where the last digit is your lucky number.
2. You can gain confidence if you make use of your lucky colours for painting your living room or bed room, or use these colours while selecting your clothes.
3. You can increase the vibrations of your personality by wearing your lucky jewels.
4. You can plan all your important activities during your important years.

CHAPTER 8

NUMBER 5

All those born on 5th, 14th and 23rd of any month are governed by number 5 and this is their ruling number.

Character

BORN ON THE 5TH OF THE MONTH:

This number is governed by the planet Mercury and it shows shrewdness, quickness, scientific pursuits, business ability, industry, intuition and diplomacy. You are active and quick; this pertains not only to physical agility but to the mental side as well. You are very skilful and have an intuitive faculty. You are equally proficient in games where you use your hands as well as your brain. You have the capacity to judge the ability of your opponents in games and know very well how to take advantage of the weak points of your opponents. You are fond of oratory and eloquence in expressing yourself. You have the capacity to pursue your objectives and know very well how to plan for achieving your aims. You are deeply interested in occult subjects and in mastering all the intricacies of abstruse subjects. You are a nervous person and therefore restless. You can be either good or bad. On the good side, you are a shrewd person and not vicious or criminal. You are fond of family life and love children. Your pleasures are mainly mental and you evaluate every thing in terms of business.

Everything you do is characterized by speed, efficiency and determination. Nothing can keep you rooted to a single spot, for you must travel far and wide to be happy and you must travel fast. You love change and variety and possess versatility.

You have a broad and tolerant view of life and will strengthen your spirit of comradeship. You will always be willing to help others in trouble but will need to maintain common sense as there will be times when others will seek to take advantage of your goodness. Religious and philosophical matters will appeal to you.

BORN ON THE 14TH OF THE MONTH:

You have all the basic characteristics explained for number 5 above, so first read them and then read your own as born on the 14th of the month.

You are practical, industrious and in many ways capable of exercising considerable patience where the more important interests of lite are concerned. Many of your desires and wishes will be associated with money. You have an urge within you to broadcast to the world your beliefs, ideas and opinions. For this reason, you would make an excellent critic.

You have an attractive personality and are liked by all. Your nature is cooperative and you do not like to provoke others. You usually occupy a good position in life and are successful in business. You are inconsistent in love and experience some romantic attachment in early years. You are fortunate in money matters.

BORN ON THE 23RD OF THE MONTH:

You have all the basic characteristics explained for number 5 above; so first read them and then read your own as born on the 23rd of the month.

You are usually popular among the opposite sex. Your fortune is near the water. You are successful in life and enjoy honour and wealth. You may get money through inheritance. You keep yourself busy in your own way. You get help from superiors and get protection from them. You are a lucky person.

You are highly emotional and changeable. Your vocabulary is extensive and you express yourself well in many ways—speaking, writing, singing, lecturing, teaching and demonstrating. You have your freedom and nothing binds you. You are quick to express your devotion and hence you gather many admirers. You have an attraction for fast moving vehicles and for fast methods of doing things.

Finance

Since number 5 is a business number, so you can expect opulence. With your shrewd characteristics, you are capable of developing your industry, carrying out your plans systematically with the result that you get good returns for the efforts you have put in. You are lucky as far as your financial position is concerned.

In order to be successful in financial matters, please refer to Chapter 15 and find out your lucky money number and start all your financial activities on that number.

Vocation

Nowadays, there are innumerable vocations and it is not possible to pinpoint any one as such. However, the vocations given below indicate the utility of your inherent abilities which, if brought into practice, will lead you to be a successful personality.

You are adaptable to the role you have to play in the drama of life. With your ability you come in contact with various classes of people and are successful in whatever you accept in life. Banking is a good business for you. The planet Mercury also shows ability for medicine and surgery. Your capacity to argue and prove your point can make you a good lawyer.

Health

The number 5 gives a very favorable reaction upon health and shows that, with normal forethought, you will have good health. Even during periods of indisposition there will be compensations and the recuperative powers will pull you through ailments that generally prove very disturbing to other people. You are, however, required to take care where food and drink are concerned. Your basic defect is your biliousness and nervousness. However, your biliousness is closely related to your psychological disturbances. Experience shows that your biliousness increases with increase in tension and the same is reduced or disappears when your nervous trouble is under control. Number 5 rules over nerves, neck, arms, ears and the respiratory system.

Marriage And Friends

There will be a strong desire for affection, but the factor of sincerity will count for a lot, and despite a natural desire for companionship previous to marriage, the commonsense view of affairs will keep this desire within bounds. Your love affairs and marriage will be productive and happiness will prevail. In some respects interests of a philosophical and religious nature will play their part and the marriage partner can be met whilst attending church, temple or a religious ceremony. There will be love and sympathy from the marriage partner and benefit for your vocational and financial matters.

You have a natural attraction towards persons born in the period between 21st September and 20th October and between 21st January and 20th February. It is therefore advisable that you find your marriage partner from this period. You also have affinity for those who are governed by numbers 1, 5, 7 and 8.

NUMBER 5 AS A HUSBAND:

You are lucky and successful in your married life. Your selection is good and usually you select a person of your own type. You love your partner. You expect neatness and cleanliness from your partner and also desire that your partner should share with you the enjoyment of life. You are proud of your wife and like to see her well dressed. In return, you prove yourself to be a good husband. You love your children and are fond of home. Even when you travel, you are very much attracted towards home and are eager to return early and be among the members of your family. You are liberal in spending on clothing and other wants of the members of your family and furnish your house with good taste.

NUMBER 5 AS WIFE:

You have interest at home as well as outside. You have many activities and manage them well. You like tidiness and, though you seldom do your own work, you get it done through your commanding personality.

Friends

Your best friends are those who are governed by numbers 1, 3, 4, 5, 7 and 8.

Fortunate Days

Your lucky days are Wednesday, Fridays and Saturdays.

Lucky Colours

Your lucky colours are white and green. You should not use red.

Lucky Jewels And Stones

Your lucky jewels are emerald and diamond. You may use sapphire also.

Important Years In Life

Your important years are 5, 14, 23, 32, 41, 50, 59, 68, 77 etc. Mostly good and auspicious events take place during these years. You will either get your graduation, or first job or your promotion or a house or your marriage, or any other events which is considered auspicious

Your good qualities and drawbacks are as under:

Good Qualities	*Drawbacks*
Co-operation	Lack of perseverance
Practicability	Sscepticism
Shrewdness	unrealiability
Vigilance	

Important:

Please also refer to the month you are born in. Combine your characteristics, lucky days, colours and jewels shown by your number and also by the month you are born in and then find out the common factors and arrive at the final conclusion.

However, if you do not find any common factor, then follow the lucky days, colours and the jewels as shown by your Ruling Number and not by the month.

The study of numbers is nothing but the study of psycho-analysis. The deep-rooted feelings, sentiments, emotions, ambitions and abilities are best represented by numbers. You can take advantage of your abilities and try to overcome your drawbacks so that life will be easy and successful.

Fadic Number 5

Fadic number is the single number arrived at after totalling all the numbers in your complete birth-date. If the total of your complete birth-date is 5, it shows the following:

Your life will be a constant succession of changes, mostly for the better, but your basic attitude will lack definition and reveal no clear-cut ambition. Throughout life, documents will have great importance for you—much depends upon new agreements, contracts and commercial transactions. Difficulties will arise from a talkative and unreliable attitude. Your financial matters will improve by travel.

As regards friendships, you will spend more time in the company of younger people. Partnerships based on mental affinity will be most important. Contacts with someone important will be maintained at a distance through correspondence and despite the special separation this association will have significant consequences.

You are intensely knowledgeable but examination will show that your grasp is light and superficial, since you lack the patience to pursue a deep study.

Important Note

In order to get full benefit of the things explained herein and to achieve success in life you should act upon the following recommendations:

1. You should do all your important work on your lucky days and dates. You may try your luck in lottery by purchasing a ticket where the total of all numbers works out to your lucky number or where the last digit is your lucky number.
2. You can gain confidence if you make use of your

lucky colours for painting your living room or bed room, or use these colours while selecting your clothes.

3. You can increase the vibrations of your personality by wearing your lucky jewels.
4. You can plan all your important activities during your important years.

CHAPTER 9

NUMBER 6

All those born on 6th, 15th and 24th of any month are governed by number 6 and this is their ruling number.

Character

BORN ON THE 6TH OF THE MONTH:

This number is governed by the planet Venus which stands for love, sympathy, and adoration. You are a born artist and love for art and beauty in life have an attraction for you. You are a pleasant personality to meet. It is always charming to be with you. Your company is full of enthusiasm, energy and charm. Your talk is interesting and lively. Others are required to put aside their ideas of morality and social conduct if they have to understand you and appreciate your discussions and feelings. You have vitality, warmth, beauty and attraction. You are fond of music, dancing and poetry. You love to have a life full of ease and luxuries, money and happiness. You prefer spending to saving. You will have rich clothes, jewellery, perfumes and all sorts of beautiful things.

You are necessarily a loving type and have a feeling of kinship and humanity. You will therefore not desert your friends and always like to understand the grievances and difficulties of others, your approach is always considerate. You prefer joy to gloom and have the capacity to carry others with you to participate in the moments of enjoyment. Your outlook is bright and vivacious.

You are deeply attached to your family and home and one of your dreams is to make everyone of your family happy. Your entire existence is a series of progressive steps for every experience you have is an embodiment of the law of education. You learn at every step, and therefore your advance in wisdom is rapid.

BORN ON THE 15TH OF THE MONTH:

You have all the basic characteristics explained for number 6 above, so first read them and then your own as born on the 15th of the month.

You have a good intelligence and a good memory. You are fit for responsible positions and can be an ambassador, consular, governor, etc. You are very ambitious and boastful but hasty and proud by nature. You are interested in the lower types of occultism. You also have interest in art and music. You appear to be gentle but have very strong convictions. You have a habit of worrying constantly and leading a melancholy life. Your fate is to make sacrifices for others.

Your home, family and friends form a circle of affectionate ties which bind you, but in no sense do they distress you. You can be a leader in public speaking, lecturing, and in writing and radio work.

BORN ON THE 24TH OF THE MONTH:

You have all the basic characteristics explained for number 6 above; so first read them and then read your own as born on the 24th of the month.

You are fortunate in getting assistance from people of high rank. You benefit through the opposite sex. Your prosperity is after marriage and you are likely to marry a rich person. You succeed in speculation and enjoy good monetary status. You define the line between personal and social matters. You are methodic in your ideas. You possess a strong ego and sometimes try to force your opinions on others. You feel that no greater delight can come to anyone than through learning and you are the teacher. You like to be surrounded by the beautiful things of life and you make a strong effort to get them.

Finance

You are not attracted towards money, and accumulation of wealth is not your aim in life. All your interest is directed towards attaining pleasures and gratifying your desires. You therefore spend your earnings on whatever attracts you. You also never repent having spent your money on art, which may not ultimately bring you monetary rewards. Opulence therefore is a rarity with you but you somehow have the knack to make both ends meet and have the minimum comforts you want. You may sometimes be lucky in having windfalls.

In order to be successful in your financial matters, please refer to Chapter 15 and find out your lucky money number and start all your financial activities on that number.

Vocation

Nowadays, there are innumerable vocations and it is not possible to pinpoint any one as such. However, the vocations given below indicate the utility of your inherent abilities which, if brought into practice, will lead you to be a successful personality in life.

You will shine as an interior decorator, architect, jeweller, musician, hotel manager or a confectioner. You can be equally successful as a broker, estate broker or as a commission agent.

Health

On the whole you are a healthy person and bad health does not trouble you. However, you are susceptible to epidemic fever and influenza. Occasionally, you are prone to nervousness but not in a chromic way.

Marriage And Friends

You have a natural attraction towards those born in the period between 21st August and 20th September and between 21st December and 20th January. Therefore it is advisable that you choose your partner from this period. You also have an affinity for those who are governed by the numbers 2, 3, 6 and 9.

NUMBER 6 AS HUSBAND:

You are attracted to marriage and usually marry early in life. You expect your partner to be neat and have charm and grace. Yours is usually a large family with many children. You love your children and home. You are very kind, generous and devoted. Though you create a lively atmosphere in the house, you somehow find it difficult to meet all the necessities of the members of your family. This may sometimes create unpleasantness and make you unhappy in your married life. Art is everything to you and you remain impractical in not understanding the material values of a successful life.

It is necessary for you to control sudden emotions; otherwise attachments of an unsatisfactory nature will be formed which would disturb your married life. If you can differentiate between fascination and true love, real happiness, both before and after marriage, is your lot.

NUMBER 6 AS WIFE:

You never resort to divorce and endure extreme hardship rather than desert your mate. You are a devoted mother and a loving wife, satisfied with your husband's efforts on your behalf. You love domestic life and are a perfect housewife.

Friends

Your best friends are those who are governed by numbers 2, 3, 6 and 9

Fortunate Days

Your lucky days are Mondays, Tuesdays, Thursdays and Fridays.

Lucky Colours

You should use all shades of blue, rose and pink. It is advised that you avoid yellow.

Lucky Jewels And Stones

You can use turquoise, emerald, pearl and diamond

Important Years In Life

Your important years are 6, 15, 24, 33, 42, 51, 60, 69, 78 etc. Mostly good and auspicious events take place during these years. You will either get your graduation, or first job or your promotion or a house or your marriage, or any other events which is considered auspicious

Your good qualities and drawbacks are as under:

Good Qualities	*Drawbacks*
Harmony	Absence of foresight
Love	Interference
Peace	Moodiness
Strong memory	Timidity

Important:

Please also refer to the month you are born in. Combine your characteristics, lucky days, colours and jewels as shown by your number and also by the month you are born in and then find out the common factors and arrive at the final conclusion. If there is no common factor then follow the lucky days, colours and jewels as shown by your Ruling number and not by the month.

The study of numbers is nothing but the study of psycho-analysis. The deep-rooted feelings, sentiments, emotions, ambitions and abilities are best represented by numbers. You can take advantage of your abilities and try to overcome your drawbacks so that life will be easy and successful.

Fadic Number 6

Fadic number is the single number arrived at after totalling all the numbers in your complete birth-date. If the total of your complete birth date is 6, it shows the following:

You have a harmonious and friendly background with sentimental attachments. The work done in partnership will prove much more successful than that undertaken independently. You will become increasingly popular with your associates. As regards health, watch carefully for throat ailments and chills.

Important Note

In order to get full benefit of the things explained herein and to achieve success in life you should act upon the following recommendations:

1. You should do all your important work on your lucky days and dates. You may try your luck in lottery by

purchasing a ticket where the total of all numbers works out to your lucky number or where the last digit is your lucky number.

2. You can gain confidence if you make use of your lucky colours for painting your living room or bed room, or use these colours while selecting your clothes.
3. You can increase the vibrations of your personality by wearing your lucky jewels.
4. You can plan all your important activities during your important years.

CHAPTER 10

NUMBER 7

All those born on 7th, 16th and 25th of any month are governed by number 7 and this is their ruling number.

Character

BORN ON THE 7TH OF THE MONTH:

You are governed by the planet Neptune and have the same qualities as those of number 2 which is governed by the planet Moon. You have individuality and are original and independent. You are restless by nature and are fond of change. You like to visit foreign countries and become interested in far off lands. You have peculiar ideas about religion and dislike following the beaten track. Number 7 is a spiritual number and Supreme Consciousness is developed in you. You are like a free bird and like to break the traditional bondage and restrictions. It is possible that the greatest of the prophets and spiritualists have the planet Neptune dominating them. Your behaviour is a mystery to others and you are many times absent minded. You think logically and achieve great aims. You are stubborn and disregard the opinion of others. You have a good talent for earning money. In general, you are somewhat indifferent and care little for materialistic things. You desire the best or none at all. You are sensitive and hide your real feelings by appearing indifferent. You dislike mingling with common people. You prefer to spend your hours with your favourite book. When your opinion is solicited, you speak with authority.

You are frank and outspoken with a very strong desire for liberty and freedom of thought and action. Under normal circumstances you will adhere to the ordinary customs and conventions of life, but should affairs become too monotonous, or should there be any degree of what appears to you to be unfair restriction or limitation a spirit of rebellion will occur and you will then say and do things and bring about changes without letting the immediate results affect you too strongly. You are naturally happy, energetic and optimistic but you will need to control impulsive and hasty inclinations which may lead you to restlessness. You are naturally self-reliant and you can inspire others by the example you set.

BORN ON THE 16TH OF THE MONTH:

You have all the basic characteristics explained for number 7 above, so first read them and then read your own as born on the 16th of the month.

You are rather easy going and do not like to work hard. You are good-humored and generous. You are very sensitive and emotional. You get upset very soon and equally soon are you pleased. You are frequently indisposed. You are fortunate in getting good and successful children. However there is some sort of sorrow in married life. You appear to be calm but your mind is always in turmoil and sometimes you are short-tempered. You will not disclose your nervousness and are slow in taking decisions. You do not like interference.

You are modest and do not like to show off your strength. The subtler things in life appeal to you. On the light side you choose detective stories, on the heavy side, you find an interest in all mystic things. You are clever, alert and intellectual. You have a great magnetism for people but you are not too quick to part with your affections. You should learn to relax with the lighter pleasures of the mind and spirit. Too much concentration inclines you to depression; this you must ovoid. You are courageous and will always face odds and do your best to overcome them.

BORN ON THE 25TH OF THE MONTH:

You have all the basic characteristics explained for number 7 above; so first read them and then read your own as born on the 25th of the month.

You are a jack of all trades, but master of none. You are interested in several subjects but do not have the capacity to go into details. Your knowledge, therefore, is very shallow. You like to travel and have connections with foreign countries. You are honest, faithful and good natured. But you are fickle-minded and inconsistent. Your memory is good and you make a good orator and teacher.

You are imaginative, quiet and somewhat of a sphinx to your family and acquaintances. Your life is one of sincerity, loyalty, honesty and all the finer virtues. You are a seeker of truth, Be advised. Do not ever lose or sacrifice your high ideas.

Finance

Usually, you have a number of changes in life. It is, therefore, difficult for you to amass wealth. However, the number 7 is a mystic number and you can be well placed in life if you find a job of your choice. In that case you can be a wealthy person with all amenities and comforts.

In order to be successful in financial matters please refer to Chapter 15 and find out your lucky money number and start all your financial activities on that number.

Vocation

Nowadays, there are innumerable vocations and it is not possible to pinpoint any one as such. However the vocations given below indicate the utility of your inherent abilities which if brought into practice will lead you to be a successful personality.

Your love of sea-travel and interest in foreign countries can make you a successful merchant, exporter or importer. You can as well deal in dairy products, fishery, chemical industry and other products such as soap, etc. You can also study medicine and surgery.

Health

Your main trouble is your nervous constitution, and so all your illnesses will be due to your nervousness. You are liable to suffer from faulty blood circulation, stomach disorders and fever. There is a possibility that your health will suffer due to over-activity, and over-excitement. You should therefore, always try to regulate periods of work with periods of physical and mental rest.

Marriage And Friends

You have a natural attraction towards persons born in the period from 21st October and 20th November and from 19th February to 20th March. It is, therefore, advisable that you find your marriage partner from this period. You also have affinity for those who are governed by numbers 1, 3, 4, 5, 7 and 8.

NUMBER 7 AS HUSBAND:

You are very emotional and understand the feelings of your wife. You are very considerate and will never try to impose your ideas on your wife. You are liberal, fond of picnics, travels and the cinema. You are a spendthrift and like to live lavishly. Your family is moderate in size and have all the comforts of life.

NUMBER 7 AS WIFE:

You are very moody and your behaviour is unpredictable. You are very uneasy and get easily disturbed over small matters. You are good at entertaining friends and you like to invite people for parties or dinner. You expect your husband to look after you all the time.

Friends

Your best friends are those who are governed by numbers 1, 3, 4, 5, 7, 8 and 9.

Fortunate Days

Your lucky days are Sundays, Mondays, Wednesdays and Thursdays. You should take your decisions and act on these days especially when the date is also 7th or 16th or 25th of the month.

Lucky Colours

You should use all shades of green and yellow.

Lucky Jewels And Stones

Your lucky jewels are topaz and emerald, and your lucky stones are moonstone and cat's eye.

Important Years In Life

Your important years are 7, 16, 25, 34, 43, 52, 61, 70 and 79 etc. Mostly good and auspicious events take place during these years. You will either get your graduation, or first job or your promotion or a house or your marriage, or any other events which is considered auspicious.

Your good qualities and drawbacks are as under:

Good Qualities	*Drawbacks*
Austerity	Despondency
Peace	Diffidence
Reflection	Restlessness
Serenity	Whimsicality
Tolerance	

Important:

Please also refer to the month you are born in. Combine your characteristics, lucky days, colours and jewels as shown by your number and also by the month you are born in and then find out the common factors and arrive at the final conclusion. However, if you do not find any common factor, then follow the lucky days, jewels etc. as shown by your Ruling number and not by the month.

The study of numbers is nothing but the study of psycho-analysis. The deep-rooted feelings, sentiments, emotions, ambitions and abilities are best represented by numbers. You can take advantage of your abilities and try to overcome your drawbacks so that life will be easy and successful.

Fadic Number 7

Fadic number is the single number arrived at after totalling all the numbers in your complete birth-date. If the total of your complete birth-date is 7, it shows the following:

Your life is a challenge. You will find it difficult to carry on without a sharply defined goal in sight. There will be too many plans, too much intervention and too little direction.

Unanimity will always seem to be lacking. It will be necessary for you to see that life does not deteriorate into a chain of unrelated experiences about which you show too little initiative. As regards finance, you are advised to double check on new schemes.

Important Note

In order to get full benefit of the things explained herein and to achieve success in life you should act upon the following recommendations:

1. You should do all your important work on your lucky days and dates. You may try your luck in lottery by purchasing a ticket where the total of all numbers works out to your lucky number or where the last digit is your lucky number.
2. You can gain confidence if you make use of your lucky colours for painting your living room or bed room, or use these colours while selecting your clothes.
3. You can increase the vibrations of your personality by wearing your lucky jewels.
4. You can plan all your important activities during your important years.

CHAPTER 11

NUMBER 8

All those born on 8th, 17th and 26th of any month are governed by number 8 and this is their ruling number.

Character

BORN ON THE 8TH OF THE MONTH:

This number is governed by the planet Saturn and shows an extreme sense of discipline, steadfastness, constancy and dutifulness. You are, therefore, sober and of the solitary type. You are a lover of classical music but mostly of melancholy type. When it comes to art, you love landscapes, natural scenery and flowers. Number 8 is considered to be a balance wheel to character. You are a pessimist. You prefer solitude to company. You shun society rather than court it. You are cautious about the future and you take decisions very carefully. You are a prudent person, wise and sober. You are never enthusiastic and more or less gloomy and melancholy. You are also ambitious and preserving. You are capable of enormous efforts for the attainment of desired objects. You are sceptical and analytical. You are creative, productive and dominating. You are likely to be misunderstood. You usually feel lonely at heart. You understand the weak and oppressed and treat them in a warm hearted manner. You are a born manager who can keep others busy. You admire fair play and are willing to pay a fair compensation. You have a good memory for names and faces.

The organisation of the many departments of life needs power, force and strength—and these you possess to a strongly marked degree. You have the ability to handle all material affairs with great ease and you specialise in the careful, honest and efficient manipulation of money matters. When others need help, they turn to you, for you have a deep understanding of the problems of other people, and a deep insight into the cause of their troubles.

There will be a more or less natural gravitation towards the holding of positions of authority and trust but you should not permit others to shift unfair burdens of responsibility on to your shoulders and then take the credit and benefit for themselves. You can always work hard and long and will set an example to others. For this reason you will also experience difficulties when you want others to carry out work for you. Sometimes you will know what it is to feel depressed and unhappy, and will temporarily lose heart and wonder if there is any thing in life worth working for. During these periods do not shun the company of others but take part in social affairs.

BORN ON THE 17TH OF THE MONTH:

You have all the basic characteristics explained for the number 8 above; so first read them and then read your own as born on the 17th of the month.

You are a good organiser and a good thinker. You have a creative and constructive mind. You are a lover of peace and a philanthropist. You are attracted towards occultism and mysticism. You are courageous and proud. You possess strong individualism. You are highly intelligent and clever. As regards emotions, you are clam. At times, you are generous to a fault, and at other times very stingy. You are interested in research and seek knowledge. You are conservative and dominating.

Your own timidity may sometimes shock you. This is because you are used to leadership and sometimes lose sight of the fact that deep within, you are a sensitive human being. When you extend your best efforts there is almost nothing of which you are not capable. Success comes to you through your own ideas and a clever way of presenting them to the market place of the world.

BORN ON THE 26TH OF THE MONTH:

You have all the basic characteristics explained for the number 8 above; so first read them and then read your own as born on the 26th of the month.

You want to enjoy life without doing anything. You are sluggish and lethargic. You revel in wine and women and are fickle-minded. You are careless about the number of children. You are lucky in money matters and get easy money. You are smart but lack positiveness. You like to put up a good appearance but have a worrying nature. You have problems in love affairs.

You are concerned with the welfare of your home and loved ones. Big deals have a fascination for you and you are happy when engaged in any form of corporate employment or direction. Your executive ability can be put to good use as a club counsellor or in your own business. Although you are affectionate, you are not particularly demonstrative. You are endowed with a vital and energetic nature.

Finance

The peculiarity of number 8 is the delay in life in all matters. Naturally, in financial matters also, there is delay, and stability is achieved at a very late age. You have to work hard but rarely succeed in getting opulence. You have therefore to avoid number 8 playing a part in your life.

instead, choose number 3 or 7 for all your important actions and moves in life. However, if your experience shows that 8 is your lucky number then you can insist on that number only. Wealth and prosperity is not difficult if number 8 is lucky for you. In that case you can also try your luck in lotteries or in horse racing.

In order to be successful in financial matters, please refer to Chapter 15 and find out your lucky money number and start all your financial activities on that number.

Vocation

Nowadays, there are innumerable vocations and it is not possible to pinpoint any one as such. However, the vocations given below indicate the utility of your inherent abilities which, if brought into practice, will lead you to be a successful personality.

Subjects suitable for you are occult sciences, chemistry, physics, medicine and also higher mathematics. You can be successful in industries dealing with coal mines, timber, etc. and in construction companies. However, as stated earlier you have to strive hard in your career; your labour will bear fruit only in the later years of life.

Health

Your main health defects are nervousness, irritation, and trouble with the legs, teeth and ears. Paralysis and rheumatism are likely. You are a bilious type and many times suffer from chronic melancholia. It is very interesting to note that the delaying characteristic in your life is also observed in your sickness. The ailments you suffer from also take a long time to cure. Varicose veins and hemorrhoids are a common tendency of a strong 8 personality.

Marriage And Friends

You have a natural attraction towards persons born in the period between 21st April and 20th May and between 21st August and 20th September. It is, therefore, advisable that you select your marriage partner from this period. You also have affinity for those who are governed by numbers 4, 5, 7 and 8.

NUMBER 8 AS HUSBAND:

Basically, you only have a weak desire to get married. You prefer loneliness and like to be left to yourself. You have less attraction for the opposite sex. Usually you try to postpone your marriage with the result that if at all you marry it will be at a very late stage. You also find it difficult to choose your partner. You prefer seclusion to social gatherings, as a result of which you make your married life miserable. You are very orthodox in your views and do not allow your wife to adopt modern ideas in dress at home or in public places. The natural result is disappointment on the part of the wife and hatred for her husband. If, however, you have a desire to be successful in married life, you should prefer a person who is also interested in deep and serious studies and likes to devote herself to philosophy and occult subjects.

NUMBER 8 AS WIFE:

You have a masculine personality. You are capable and systematic. You enjoy your family life and like to make sacrifices for your children and for the ambitions of your husband. Your fault is that you lack feminine warmth, sentiment and delicacy.

Friends

Your best friends are those who are governed by numbers 3, 4, 5, 7 and 8.

Fortune Days

Your lucky days are Wednesdays, Thursdays and Saturdays.

Lucky Colours

You should wear dark grey, dark blue, purple and black colours.

Lucky Jewels And Stones

Your lucky jewels are sapphire, black pearl, black diamond and your lucky stones are cat's eye and amethyst.

Important Years In Life

Your important years are 8, 17, 26, 35, 44, 53, 62 and 71 etc. Mostly good and auspicious events take place during these years. You will either get your graduation, or first job or your promotion or a house or your marriage, or any other events which is considered auspicious.

Your good qualities and drawbacks are as under:

Good Qualities	*Drawbacks*
Authority	Cynicism
Methodical	Delay
Practical	Vindictiveness
Steady	Nervousness
Systematic	Laziness

Important:

Please also refer to the month you are born in. Combine your characteristics, lucky days, colours and jewels as shown by your number and also by the month you are born in and then find out the common factors and arrive at the final conclusion. However, if you do not find any common factor, then follow the lucky days, jewels etc. as shown by your Ruling number and not by the month.

The study of numbers is nothing but the study of psycho-analysis. The deep-rooted feelings, sentiments, emotions, ambitions and abilities are best represented by numbers. You can take advantage of your abilities and try to overcome your drawbacks so that life will be easy and successful.

Fadic Number 8

Fadic number is the single number arrived at after totalling all the numbers in your complete birth-date. If the total of your complete birth date is 8, it shows the following:

You will have a extremely busy life with the best results brought about through perseverance. The fact that you have to wait to reap the fruit of your actions will be forgotten in the growing responsibilities which will inevitably be assumed. It will be conservative methods which will prove advantageous. As regards financial matters, gain will be slow and is not likely to be achieved through speculation. Older people will prove to be helpful. As regards occupation, real estate, insurance, building, mining, heavy industries will prove beneficial.

Special Observation About Number 8

It has been observed in the study of numerology that those who are governed by the number 8 are always haunted by this number. This number goes on establishing its dominance in the career of the individual and this number will always recur on several important occasions. For instance, supposing you start writing an important letter, you will find that the date is 8th, 17th or 26th of the month. If you enter into a contract or purchase a new car or a house, the date will be usually in the series of 4 or 8. As a general rule, number 8 indicates delays and difficulties in life though it has other positive and good qualities. You will find that the events that have taken place on these days have created hardships or obstacles in your progress. In that case it is better to avoid these dates while deciding upon important moves and instead you would select dates in the series 3 or 7.

I have observed that those who are born in April and August (4th and 8th of the month) and also have dates in the series of 4 and 8 have children who are dominated by either of the two numbers. At least one of the children is born in these series.

An Interesting Experience Of Delay Shown By The Number 8

Once a retired person called on me and informed me that he had retired three years back but still he had not got his pension and his case was not finalised even after three years. In fact, he was working as an officer in the same department where pension matters were settled. He had visited his office several times during the last three years and every time his juniors in that office promised to settle the case within a week's time. He then asked me when his case would be settled and he would get his pension. In Numerology there is a system with the help of which we can solve such questions. I just asked him to write down his question and after his doing so, the question was solved in the numerical way and the final digit arrived at was 8. I immediately informed him that the number indicated delay and he would have to wait for some time more to get his pension but how long could not be predicted.

For the next two years he used to visit me and the delay shown by the number 8 was really trying his patience. After about a year thereafter he called on me with a packet of sweets and gave me the happy news that he had received his pension. But till the last moment number 8 played the delaying game and the old man had to go to Bombay to take his pension when he was informed that it had been sent to Poona by money order only two days earlier. After returning to poona, he was told that the money order had been returned to Bombay office. This is really an extraordinary case.

Important Note

In order to get full benefit of the things explained herein and to achieve success in life you should act upon the following recommendations:

1. You should do all your important work on your lucky days and dates. You may try your luck in lottery by purchasing a ticket where the total of all numbers works out to your lucky number or where the last digit is your lucky number.
2. You can gain confidence if you make use of your lucky colours for painting your living room or bed room, or use these colours while selecting your clothes.
3. You can increase the vibrations of your personality by wearing your lucky jewels.
4. You can plan all your important activities during your important years.

CHAPTER 12

NUMBER 9

All those born on 9th, 18th and 27th of any month are governed by number 9 and this is their ruling number.

Character

BORN ON THE 9TH OF THE MONTH:

This number is governed by the planet Mars and shows aggression, resistance, courage, dash and quickness. You are considered a fighter. You are always aggressive in all your acts and will not stop till you achieve your end. You have the capacity to fight even against all adverse elements and circumstances. You do not know defeat. You would have either victory or death. It is said that the great emperor Napoleon Bonaparte was a believer in numerology and had a battalion of soldiers who were pure Martians. You are not very tactful or delicate in your talk, but your intention is good and your vigorous manner should not be misunderstood as rough behavior,

You are fiery and dashing and do not have sickly sentiments. You have audacity and vigour. You are also fond of games and vigorous exercise. When the date of the month is 9 and the total of all the birth-date is also 9, you are governed by a strong number 9 and your Mars is very powerful. In such a case, you have strong sexual passions and you are attracted towards the opposite sex. You are prepared to go through any ordeal to gratify your desire.

You are a brave person to whom conflict does not bring the thought of danger. You are exceedingly devoted to your friends and will fight for them. You have sympathy and consideration for the weak. You love children and animals. You take delight in showing mercy to others. You like the healing profession. You are backed by self-control, moral courage and the power of forgiveness. Your psychological aptitude is remarkable and under all circumstances you prove your strength of will and exhibit courage.

You have an unusual psychic sense and are inclined to have occult experiences. Travel will broaden your outlook and should play an important role in your life. You will travel wide and the road will eventually lead to tolerance, sympathy and a universal love. You are thoughtful, reflective and studious. Many of your thoughts and ideas will be in advance of those around you. In fact, you will find that those with whom you associate will often look to you for advice regarding their problems. Discretion will be required regarding the taking on of obligations and liabilities, especially of a financial character, where friends and relatives are concerned. You have some very strong likes and dislikes and will be very firm where your principles, convictions and lines of action are concerned, and will put up great resistance when others try to force you to do things that are against your own inclinations.

BORN ON THE 18TH OF THE MONTH:

You have all the basic characteristics explained for the number 9 above; so first read them and then read your own as born on the 18th of the month.

You have tenacity and will-power which will overcome any difficulty. You are not as dashing as number 9, but you are fearless and courageous. Your strong health makes you passionate. You inherit property from your father. You have a disciplined mind and like to help others. You are painstaking with good judgement, and wise. You have a very vivid imagination and will be able to recall clearly and easily many of the events which have occurred in the past. You should utilise the knowledge gained from past experiences to deal with and to regulate present affairs. Matters to do with the home and the family side of life will always be of great importance to you and will influence many of your decisions and actions. You can also do many things yourself towards creative domestic comfort and making others feel at home when they are in your surroundings. You have a very good memory, much tenacity of thought and purpose which enables you to use your imagination to create publicity either for yourself or for others.

BORN ON THE 27TH OF THE MONTH:

You have all the basic characteristics explained for number 9 above; so first read them and then read your own as born on the 27th of the month.

On the whole you are a conflicting personality. You are confident and like to do something for those whose life is miserable or those who are in any way handicapped. You can develop a spiritual personality and can practice spiritual healing. On the other side you are fond of the opposite sex and can develop illicit contacts and create scandals. Sometimes you create unhappiness in your married life. You are very sensitive and moody and your actions are unpredictable.

The course of your life includes a very wide variety of experiences. You are an intellectual, and a sympathetic and deep thinker. Long range projects fascinate you and all matters of distance and dimension intrigue you. A career dealing with travel, railroads, ships, telegraphy or television should prove successful for you.

Finance

You are lucky in your monetary affairs and earn far more than an average person. You are also very liberal while spending, especially when it concerns your sweet heart. You enjoy all the comforts that money can buy.

In order to be successful in financial matters, please refer to Chapter 15 and find out your lucky money number and start all your financial activities on that number.

Vocation

Nowadays, there are innumerable vocations and it is not possible to pinpoint any one as such. However, the vocations given below indicate the utility of your inherent abilities which if brought into practice will lead you to be a successful personality.

People with your number are found in all walks of life but you will be more suitable for the army and professions where there is full scope for your aggression and courage. In the army you rise to high positions; in politics you will be eminent and in business you will exhibit your dashing and pushing nature. You can be a good doctor or a chemist or a businessman dealing in iron and steel.

Health

Your main health defect arises from heat and you are susceptible to troubles such as piles, fevers, small pox, etc. You are also likely to suffer from kidney or bladder stone problems. Throat trouble, bronchitis, laryngitis also trouble you.

Marriage And Friends

You have a natural attraction towards persons born in the period between 21st July and 20th August and between 21st

November and 20th December. It is, therefore, advisable that you select your partner from this period. You also have affinity for those who are governed by numbers 3, 6 and 9.

NUMBER 9 AS HUSBAND:

Your robust health and strong circulation of blood make you passionate and enthusiastic about married life. You are fond of a good looking partner and like her to be submissive and passive to your sexual desires. You are fond of family and children and like to have a good house. You usually lead a good married life in spite of your hot-tempered nature and eccentricities. You have a romantic mental picture of what you want in your wife. This mental picture demands perfection. The most difficult thing in married life is to satisfy your romantic conception of physical love. You have a voracious appetite and your wife with her devotion should harmonize with you physically. Usually, you are suspicious about your wife.

As a result of marriage, you will find it easier to bring about a realisation of your hopes and wishes. Your wife will prove to be invaluable in these respects

NUMBER 9 AS WIFE:

You will be a wonderful wife for an ambitious person. You are a witty and clever conversationalist with a wonderful social presence. You will assist your husband in his business. You may also start your own activity and add to the family income. You will be happy if married to a passionate and possessive man.

Friends

Your best friends are those who are governed by the numbers 1, 2, 3, 4, 6, 7 and 9.

Fortunate Days

Your lucky days are Mondays, Tuesdays and Fridays.

Lucky Colours

You should use all shades of red, white and yellow.

Lucky Jewels And Stones

Your lucky jewels are topaz, pearl and ruby and your lucky stones are blood-stones and garnet.

Important Years In Life

Your important years are 9, 18, 27, 36, 45, 54, 63, 72 etc. Mostly good and auspicious events take place during these years. You will either get your graduation, or first job or your promotion or a house or your marriage, or any other events which is considered auspicious

Your good qualities and drawbacks are as under:

Good Qualities	*Drawbacks*
Activity	Destruction
Courage	Erratic
Dash	Hot-tempered
Energy	Impatient
Enthusiasm	Quarrelsome

Important:

Please also refer to the month you are born in. Combine your characteristics, lucky days, colours and jewels as shown by your number and also by the month you are born in and then find out the common factors and arrive at the final conclusion. However, if you do not find any common factor, then follow the lucky days, jewels etc. as shown by your Ruling number and not by the month.

The study of numbers is nothing but the study of psycho-analysis. The deep-rooted feelings, sentiments, emotions, ambitions and abilities are best represented by numbers. You can take advantage of your abilities and try to over come your drawbacks so that life will be easy and successful.

Fadic Number 9

Fadic number is the single number arrived at after totalling all the numbers in your complete birth-date. If the total of your complete birth-date is 9, it shows the following:

You are keen to make bold moves. Naturally, these will arouse much opposition and quite often there will be heated scenes. However, with a little control you should be able to make good progress. You can look forward to a year of increased activity. Your plans should always be very constructive, and extravagant outlays should be kept in check. You will be engaged in occupations concerned with tools and instruments of great precision. You can also do well in science, research and teaching

Important Note

In order to get full benefit of the things explained herein and to achieve success in life you should act upon the following recommendations:

1. You should do all your important work on your lucky days and dates. You may try your luck in lottery by purchasing a ticket where the total of all numbers works out to your lucky number or where the last digit is your lucky number.
2. You can gain confidence if you make use of your

lucky colours for painting your living room or bed room, or use these colours while selecting your clothes.

(3) You can increase the vibrations of your personality by wearing your lucky jewels.

(4) You can plan all your important activities during your important years.

SUMMARY CHART OF NUMBERS

No.	Characteristics	Finance	Vocation	Health Defects	Marriage Partner born between	Friends	Lucky Days	Lucky Colours	Lucky Jewels	Important Years
1	Originality, Activity, Energy, Brilliance	Good luck	Ambassador Surgeon Head of Dept.	Sun stroke Eye sight Heart trouble	21st July to 20th Aug. 21st Nov. to 20th Dec. Nos. 1, 3, 4, 5, 7	1, 3, 4, 5 7, 9	Sunday Monday Thursday	Gold, Yellow Orange, Purple	Ruby, Emerald Moonstone Pale green stone	1, 10, 19, 28, 37, 46, 55, 64, 73.
2	Unsteady, Fickle-minded, High imagination Lover of change.	Mediocre luck	Author, Painter, Clerk	Poor blood circulation	21st oct. to 20th Nov. 19th Feb. to 20th Mar. Nos. 2, 4, 6	2, 4 6, 9	Monday Tuesday Friday	White, Cream, Blue	Pearl, Diamond, Moonstone, Agale	2, 11, 20, 29, 38, 47, 56, 65, 74.
3	Confidence, Dignity, Prestige, Honour.	Good luck	Minister, Judge Administrator	Chest and lungs disorder	21st June to 20th July 21st Oct. to 20th Nov. Nos. 1, 3, 6, 7, 9	1, 3, 5, 6, 7, 8, 9	Tuesday Thursday Friday	Yellow, Violet, Purple, Green	Topaz, Amethyst, Cat's eye	3, 12, 21, 30, 39, 48, 57, 66, 75.
4	Energy, Force, Revolutionary.	Good	Transport Electricity Machinery	Knees, feet, Urinary infection	19th Feb. to 20th Mar. 21st Oct. to 20th Nov. Nos. 1, 2, 4, 7, 8	1, 2, 4, 5, 7, 8, 9	Sunday Monday Saturday	Elect. blue, Elect. gray White, Maroon	Diamond Coral, Pearl	4, 13, 22, 31, 40, 49, 58, 67, 76.
5	Shrewdness, Intuition Diplomacy, Eloquence.	Good	Banking, Business, Lawyer	Biliousness Nervousness Respiration	21st Sept. to 20th Oct. 21st Jan. to 20th Feb. Nos. 1, 5, 7, 8	1, 3, 4, 5, 7, 8	Wednesday Friday Saturday	Green, White	Emerald Diamond	5, 14, 23, 32, 41, 50, 59, 68, 77.
6	Love, Sympathy, Adoration.	Mediocre	Decorator, Architect, Jeweler, Musician	Nil	21st Aug. 20th Sept. 21st Dec. to 20th Jan. Nos. 2, 3, 6, 9	2, 3, 6, 9	Monday Tuesday Thursday Friday	Blue, Rose, Pink	Turquoise, Emerald Pearl, Diamond	6, 15, 24, 33, 42, 51, 60, 69, 78.
7	Originality, Independence, Restlessness	Doubtful	Merchant, Exporter, Dairy, Fishery Medicine	Nervousness Boils Fevers	21st Oct. to 20th Nov. 19th Feb. to 20th Mar. Nos. 1, 3, 4, 5, 7, 8	1, 3, 4, 5, 7, 8, 9	Sunday Monday Wednesday Thursday	Green, Yellow	Topaz, Emerald, Moonstone, Cats eye	7, 16, 25, 34, 43, 52, 61, 70, 79.
8	Dutiful, Constant, Steadfast, Gloomy, Melancholia.	Success by hard work	Science Chemistry, Medicine Accounts	Legs, teeth, ear, Rheumatism	21st Apr. to 20th May 21st Aug. to 20th Sept. Nos. 4, 5, 7, 8	3, 4, 5, 7, 8	Wednesday Thursday Saturday	Dark Grey, Dark Blue, Purple, Black	Sapphire, Black-Pearl, Black-Diamond Cat's eye	8, 17, 26, 35, 44, 53, 62, 71, 80.
9	Dash, Aggression, Courage, Resistance.	Good	Army, Doctor Iron-Steel	Piles, fever, Kidney, Laryngitis	21st Nov. to 20th Dec. 21st July to 20th Aug. Nos. 3, 6, 9	1, 2, 3, 4, 6, 7, 9	Monday Tuesday Thursday Friday	Red, White, Yellow	Topaz, Pearl, Ruby, Garnet	9, 18, 27, 36, 45, 54, 63, 72, 81.

CHAPTER 13

THE MONTH YOU ARE BORN IN

After the date of the month the next thing to be considered is the month you are born in. Every month is influenced and dominated by a particular planet and the person born in a particular month represents the characteristics of that planet. You are, therefore, influenced by the planet shown by the individual date of the month and also by the planet represented by the month. Before arriving at the final conclusion, you have to combine the aspects shown by both the planets and then find out your friends, marriage partners, lucky jewels, stones etc.

BORN IN JANUARY

The month of January is dominated by the planet Saturn according to the Zodiacal sign and also by the Sun, being the first month of the year.

Character

You are sceptical and do not believe in any thing unless you are convinced about the facts. You do not take quick decisions unless you are sure of the result. You are very cautious and do not like to speculate. Your mind is analytical and philosophic and you think deeply. You have energy and ambition and develop perseverance. You are very studious and methodical but take everything seriously. You have few friends and feel lonely in life. You are generally misunderstood. You are independent in thought and action and do not like to be dominated by others. You always desire leadership in your enterprise, otherwise you lose interest in the work. Your ideas about beauty and social behaviour are strange and, therefore, you do not get on easily with your neighbours. You are attracted to intelligent and clever people, but never like to interfere in their affairs. You are usually disturbed by your home and family affairs and have to look after distressed or invalid relatives.

You are austere, excessively critical, fault-finding and overbearing. You are dissatisfied, no matter what the recompense. You can find something to criticize in everyone else, although others think their own accomplishments as almost perfect. You do not realise the depressing effect you have upon others. You think of yourself as exceedingly accomplished and much above your associates. You think that your criticism is superior discernment and that no one measures up to your own standards. In your heart of hearts your bosses, friends and relatives are greatly beneath you and you constantly pity them for being thus afflicted with the small minds they have.

You are exceedingly ambitious and think of the highest position as yours by right. It is remarkable that you should believe that the best should be yours

Health

Varicose veins and hemorrhoids are common problems with persons born in January. In addition nervousness, melancholia, irritation, rheumatism and biliousness also trouble you.

Marriage And Friends

Your best friends and marriage partners are those who are born between 21st December and 20th January, between 21st April and 20th May and between 21st August and 20th

September. It is, therefore, advisable that you select your marriage partner from this period. You also have a natural affinity towards those born on 8th, 17th and 26th of any month.

A JANUARY HUSBAND:

You are considerate and treat your wife and family members with the same courtesy that you accord to strangers. You are kind, generous and give without thought of return or reward. You accept marriage as a part of the domestic scheme and succeed in it because of your attitude, this contributes a great deal towards harmony at home. Your drawback is your impersonal nature which your wife feels as loss of interest in domestic life.

It is seldom that you offer anything to your family members but you expect instant obedience from your children and enthusiastic affection from your wife. You distrust everyone in the family and are always investigating if you can discover some disloyalty directed against you.

A JANUARY WIFE:

You are a fine companion, capable, intelligent, adaptable and talented. Your home is a social centre on account of your social and friendly manners. Your interests are wide and you do not like to watch how your husband spends his spare time. Though basically you are unconventional, you are kind and would rather suffer yourself than create a situation which would make others unhappy. As you are intelligent you would be appreciated as a good wife by an intelligent husband who could use your abilities for his own self.

Lucky Days

Your fortunate days are Wednesdays, Thursdays and Fridays.

You should try to act on these days for all your important moves.

Lucky Colours

You will be happy and cheerful if you use grey, violet, purple or black colours for your clothes.

Lucky Jewels And Stones

You should wear either pearls, garnets, sapphire or moon stone as your lucky jewels.

Before selecting your lucky jewels, colours and days please refer to your individual number and find out the common factor and select the final jewel or colour.

BORN IN FEBRUARY

The month of February is dominated by the planet Saturn and you are governed by Saturnian characteristics.

Character

You value honour, prestige and dignity. You are oversensitive and are easily hurt in your feelings. In spite of your large contacts in society, you have a feeling of loneliness in life. You have strong intuition and can read people instinctively. You have the capacity to keep the secrets of others and relieve their distress. You have the capacity to give excellent advice to others and be in a place of trust. You require some opportunity to show your qualities but when you get one, you surprise everyone by the hidden powers and abilities you possess. You will use your energy and ability for the good of others and usually leave a name behind by service to humanity. You will have great power over excitable people or those who are hysterical or insane and you will find yourself thrown among such types in your journey through life. You have an attraction for the mysterious and the unknown and are devoted to studies of the occult and of esoteric subjects. You are attached to your family and love the members of your house.

Health

Poor blood circulation, anaemia, palpitation and weakness of the heart, disorder of the bladder and kidneys are your main health defects. You are also liable to suffer from sore throat and difficulty with the respiratory track. You will be inclined to buy any medicines from quacks.

Marriage And Friends

Your best friends and marriage partners are those who are born between 21st January and 19th February, between 21st May and 20th June and between 21st September and 20th October. It is, therefore, advisable that you select your marriage partner and friends from this period. You also have a natural affinity towards those born on 8th, 17th and 26th of any month.

A FEBRUARY HUSBAND:

You are a loving, considerate, thoughtful and attentive husband. You love your home and spend much of your time at home. You are emotional and of a dreamy nature. Your notions are more real to you than the facts of life. You, therefore, find it difficult to cope with the realities and difficulties of life. You lack stability, strain and realism in your career. You are very sensual and can be dangerously perverted by self indulgence. Sexual satisfaction is very important to you and you seek it persistently all your life.

A FEBRUARY WIFE:

You are remarkably adapted to family life. You like a luxurious life and desire your house to be a heaven. You are a devoted, kind and sympathetic wife.

Lucky Days

Your lucky days are Wednesdays, Thursdays and Saturdays and you should plan all your important actions on these days.

Lucky Colours

You should always use violet or purple or grey colours in your clothes or paint your rooms with these colours. All shades of blue are also favourable to you.

Lucky Jewels And Stones

Your most lucky jewels are amethyst, diamond or topaz. You may also wear cat's eye.

Before selecting your lucky jewels, colours and days please refer to your individual number and find out the common factor and select the final jewel or the colour.

BORN IN MARCH

Jupiter is the ruling planet of those who are born in the month of March. Naturally you are governed by Jupiterian qualities.

Character

You are courteous, generous and broad-minded. You have a natural understanding and intuition. You are ambitious and feel that you must know your subjects well. You are loyal to your friends and generally succeed in all positions of responsibility. You are strict about law and order. You are very easy going and surrounded by false friends. You have a dual personality and your action depends upon which personality dominates you at a particular moment. You have a mystical side as well as a practical one. You like to search for the unknown and the esoteric. Although you are generous you are anxious about money matters and worry about your future monetary status. Artists, musicians and literary people are born in this month.

Health

Your sickness is mainly psychological and you usually suffer from mental depression, insomnia, nervousness etc. You also suffer from rheumatic trouble, intestinal disturbance and pain in the feet. Over anxiety often causes faulty digestion and poor blood circulation.

Marriage And Friends

Your natural attraction is for those who are born between 21st June and 20th July, Between 21st October and 20th November and 10th February and 20th March. You should, therefore, choose your partner from this period. You also have a natural attraction towards those born on the 3rd, 12th, 21st and 30th of any month.

A MARCH HUSBAND:

You are highly emotional and sensitive. You desire that every thing should be given to you without your asking for it. You never think that you should contribute something of your own when it comes to fear and enjoyment. Your passions are animal-like, strong and quick. You enjoy the company of your children and are one with them in many ways.

A MARCH WIFE:

You have a great sense of comfort and decorate your home in a luxurious way. You are beautiful and talented but spend your time in an idle way, seeking entertainment. When you are of good or robust health, you make a devoted, charming and sympathetic wife.

Lucky Days

Your lucky days are Tuesdays, Thursdays, and Fridays. You should, therefore, plan all your important actions on these days.

Lucky Colours

You should try to wear clothes of yellow, violet, purple or green colours. You may also use these colours for your drawing room or bedroom.

Lucky Jewels And Stones

Your lucky jewels are topaz, sapphire, and emerald.

Before selecting your lucky jewels, colours and days please refer to your individual number and find out the common factor and select the final jewel and colour.

BORN IN APRIL

The month of April is dominated by the planet Mars and you are governed by Martian characteristics.

Character

You are dominating, energetic, active, hot-tempered, enthusiastic and a fighter. You have a capacity to organise an industry or business. You are an independent worker and can do your job when left to yourself. You do not like any interference in your work but if subjected to interference, you will step out and let the other fellow take your place. If you keep your head cool, you can reach any heights and achieve great success in life, but your arrogance and obstinacy are factors which often create enemies and thus spoil your career. You are endowed with a strong will-power and determination, and you always have new and original schemes. However you are hasty in decision and action. Sometimes you go to extremes and create enemies due to your frank and out-spoken nature. You are usually well off in life and amass good money. You are gifted with intuition and can know what is likely to happen in the future. You are a warrior and will fight all obstacles experiencing many dangers and changes in life.

Health

Though you are of a strong constitution and energetic, you are susceptible to mild fever and inflammation. In your emotional state you are likely to take alcohol which you should avoid because you need control and not stimulation. Since you are governed by the planet Mars, your head and face are more affected than any other part of the body. Pain in the teeth, ears or eyes, rushing of blood to the head, headaches and risk of apoplexy are your health weaknesses. You seldom escape wounds to the head. You are also liable to suffer from liver, bladder and stomach troubles.

Marriage And Friends

Your most harmonious relationship is with those born between 21st March and 20th April, between 21st July and 20th August and between 21 November and 20th December. You should therefore, select your marriage partner from this period. You also have a natural affinity towards those born on 9th, 18th and 27th of any month.

AN APRIL HUSBAND:

You are romantic and want your wife to be beautiful, good and clever. You have a voracious appetite for sex and your wife has to understand how to satisfy your romantic conception of physical love. You are very dashing and courageous and look after your wife and children with love and care.

AN APRIL WIFE:

You are very energetic and enthusiastic and like to help your husband either in his work or business or would like to start your own activity. You are a good conversationalist and witty. You are efficient and a good companion. You are proud of your appearance and of your family and make others jealous by your behaviour. You need a passionate and possessive husband who would allow you to spend lavishly. Your attitude towards children is generous but not sympathetic. You are irritable and impatient and not willing to see their problems from their point of view.

Lucky Days

Your lucky days are Mondays, Tuesdays and Fridays and you should, try to take important decisions on these days.

Lucky Colours

Your lucky colours are rose, crimson or pink. You should try to make use of these colours in clothes or for your drawing room or bedroom.

Lucky Jewels And Stones

Your favourable jewels are coral, pearl and garnet.

Before selecting your lucky jewels, colours and days please refer to your individual number and find out the common factor and select the final jewel and colour.

BORN IN MAY

The month of May is governed by the planet Venus and you are dominated by Venusian characteristics.

Character

You have great power of endurance, both physical and mental and can stand great strain. You are very sociable and love society, theatres, cinema houses, picnics, travels etc. You are artistic and like to decorate your house well and also to dress well. Others take you to be richer than you usually are. In love you are generous and will make sacrifices to any extent. You are emotional and sentimental. You are a good host and have a taste for good food. You can be a good nurse, healer, public servant or head of the department by virtue of your faithfulness and loyal friendship. You will also get success in art and music because of your sense of harmony and rhythm. You are lucky in money matters and gain through association, partnership or through marriage.

Health

On the whole your health is good but you should always avoid wine, strong drinks and rich foods. You are liable to suffer from complaints of the respiratory track and kidneys and self-indulgence.

Marriage And Friends

Your most harmonious relationship is with those who are born between 21st April and 20th May, between 21st August and 20th September and between 21st December and 20th January. You also have an attraction for those born between 21st October and 20th November. You should therefore try to select your marriage partner from this period as far as possible. You also have a natural attraction towards those born on 6th, 15th, and 24th of any month.

A MAY HUSBAND:

As a husband, you are very generous, devoted and faithful.

You care for your home in spite of any outside interest. You try your best to provide good education and clothes to your children. You often marry a person of a higher economic status than your own. You are attracted to beauty and usually get a good looking wife. You find your married life enjoyable and it is never tiresome to you.

A MAY WIFE:

You are a devoted and affectionate wife. You have the capacity to endure hardships and to adapt yourself to circumstances. You are calm and reserved but at the same time sociable and everybody's friend. You make yourself dependent although you can relax on your own if necessary. You are of an easy going type and enjoy picnics, theatres and the company of friends.

Lucky Days

Your lucky days are Mondays, Tuesdays, Thursdays and Fridays. You should, therefore, make use of these days for a successful future.

Lucky Colours

Your successful colours are blue, rose and pink. You may also use these colours for your drawing room or the bedroom and in selecting your clothes.

Lucky Jewels And Stones

You can wear emerald, pearl or diamond as your lucky jewels.

Before selecting your lucky jewels, colours and days please refer to your individual number and find out the common factor.

BORN IN JUNE

The month of June is dominated by the planet Mercury and therefore you are governed by the Mercurian characteristics.

Character

The Mercurian Rashi for this month is Gemini which has the symbol of twins. The main characteristic of the person born in this month is duality and therefore you play a double role in life. It is very difficult to understand you. Sometimes you look hot-headed and sometimes you appear very cool. You may like a particular thing but at the same time you may criticise it. You are sharp, brilliant and quick and can win over your rivals. You are ambitious but hardly know what you want to achieve. Your company is enjoyable, but only when you are in the right mood, otherwise your behaviour is uncertain. One can not expect you to be constant in your ideas or plans. You are usually restless and want what you do not have. You can be successful as an actor or lawyer or in any other occupation where you are required to change your role quite often. However you will hardly admit your dual personality unless you are in a self-analytical mood. Owing to your changing moods you can hardly go in for a project where much time is required for thought and decision. You are therefore not reliable in your plans which will often be postponed until you are forced by circumstances to carry them out. You are very sensitive and find it difficult to bear any strain of worry or disturbance and experience brain exhaustion and nervousness. Even though there are many ups and downs in your life, you are not much affected by them.

Health

You are not robust in health. Your main health problems

are due to mental activity and uneasiness of mind. You therefore suffer from nervous trouble and unless you get good sleep and change of atmosphere, your nervousness will grow. You are also liable to suffer from blood disorders, weakness of the respiratory system, throat infection and sometimes skin disease.

Marriage And Friends

You have natural attraction towards people born between 21st May and 20th June, between 21st September and 20th October and between 21st January and 20th February. It is, therefore, necessary that you select your life partner and friends from these period. You also have a natural affinity towards those born on 5th, 14th and 23rd of any month.

A JUNE HUSBAND:

As a husband you are good. You are intelligent, talented and sociable. You should get a wife who will understand your interests and who is not tied to household affairs. Though you have a lot of interest in women you are not flirtatious. If you can give a direction to your activities you will be successful.

A JUNE WIFE:

You are an intelligent companion to your husband. You are always busy and like to take an active part in social life. You are not much absorbed in home affairs and you will like to make use of your energy and be active. You are of course a practical type and expect returns for your service. You adore discipline and tidiness and command obedience. Though you have conversational abilities and a romantic personality, you will never sacrifice your home and husband for your romantic life. You make a good wife to a doctor, to a lawyer or an industrialist or any one who spends most of his time with his client's and social contacts.

Lucky Days

Your lucky days are Tuesdays, Thursdays and Fridays. You should plan all your important moves on these days.

Lucky Colours

Yellow, violet, purple and green are your lucky colours. You should try to use them for your clothes or for your drawing room or bedroom.

Lucky Jewels And Stones

Your lucky jewels are sapphire and emerald.

Before selecting your lucky jewels, colours and days, please refer to your individual number and then find out the common factor.

BORN IN JULY

The month of July is governed by the planet Moon. Naturally you are dominated by the characteristics of the Moon.

Character

You have a good memory, and a lot of love for your own people. You are industrious but are inclined to speculate and desire quick money. You are very sensitive, instinctive and impressionable. You have attraction for the past. You have exaggerated ideas about your abilities. You have sympathy for those who suffer. You have the capacity to persuade people to donate generously to funds in aid of hospitals or the handicapped. Generally, the organisations managed by you have good funds and are financially sound. Your main characteristic is restlessness. You are over anxious about your financial matters but once you are well placed in life, you retain your position. You are moody, timid and uncertain. However, your strong imagination helps you to be a good musician, artist or a writer. Being sensitive, you are quickly hurt and depressed. You are usually successful in your mission in life but experience troubles at home.

Health

In order to maintain good health, you have to be very particular about your diet. Because of your disturbed stomach, you suffer from gastric trouble, rheumatism, gout and some times troubles of the respiratory track.

Marriage And Friends

Your natural attraction is for those born between 21st June and 20th July, between 21st October and 20th November and between 19th February and 20th March. You should, therefore, choose your life partner and friends from one of these periods. You also have a natural affinity towards those born on 2nd, 11th, 20th and 29th of any month.

A JULY HUSBAND:

You are on the whole good natured. You are devoted to your family and children. You like to spend most of your time at home. However, there are two types of the July husband. One is the dominating type and the other is the easy going type. The first type likes others to dance to his tune. You are very exacting and try to find fault in everything. You are critical about everything and that creates tension in the mind of your family members. Nothing satisfies you. You are constantly demanding and interfering in family routine. You are very sensual and seek constant erotic stimulation.

If you are the second type of the July husband, you are

passive, lazy and self-indulgent and marry for money and comfort. Since you are submissive you often get what you want in life.

A JULY WIFE:

You are devoted, sympathetic, adaptable and satisfied with your work, position and status. You are a good mother and love your children and family. Your presence is sanctifying and you are loved and respected by others. You have intuitive faculties and sometimes can guide your husband in his business with wonderful accuracy. However, you may also have another side when you are very moody, whimsical and chanting. This creates trouble for you as well as for others. In that case you are very possessive and demanding.

Lucky Days

Your lucky days are Sundays, Mondays, Wednesdays and Thursdays. You should take advantage of these days when taking important decisions and actions in life.

Lucky Colours

Your lucky colours are green and yellow and you should try to adopt these colours either in your clothes or while painting walls at home.

Lucky Jewels And Stones

You should wear pearl or diamond in your ring. That would help you to get confidence and achieve success in life.

Before selecting your lucky jewels, colours and days, please refer to your individual number and find out the common factor and select your final jewel, or colour or the day.

BORN IN AUGUST

The month of August is governed by the planet Sun. You are, therefore, governed by the characteristics of the Sun.

Character

You have originality, dignity, prestige and honour. You have a majestic personality which commands respect. Your assistants adore you and work willingly. You are generous and have a good understanding of human problems. In your career, you succeed and achieve the highest position. You are fond of theatres, shows, and picnics. You are usually popular due to your active nature and your ability to mix in any society. Your mission is to give life, energy and enthusiasm to the world at large. You have many talents but they are of a spontaneous nature. You have a style and a grace which influence others and attract people to you with your natural brilliance and versatility.

Health

Even though you are a happy-go-lucky fellow and normally enjoy good health, you are also susceptible to certain health problems and have to be very particular about the following diseases:

Heart trouble: Your heart trouble is a structural deformity and this can be observed even in childhood.

Weak eye sight: You have magnetic eyes but they can be weak in sight.

Over exertion: The most common trouble with you is over exertion. You should always be on your guard and not exert yourself too much.

Sun stroke: You are also susceptible to this sickness.

Marriage And Friends

You are attracted to those born between 21st July and 20th August, between 21st November and 20th December and between 21st March and 20th April. Your attraction is towards those born on the 1st, 10th, 19th and 28th of any month. You should, therefore, select your partner and friends from this period.

AN AUGUST HUSBAND

You are generous and desire your wife to shine in society. You have a kind and loving disposition and a great heart. You are proud of your family and give them the best of every thing. Your love is deep and romantic. You expect your family members to dance to your tune and will not tolerate disrespect. Your opinions are fixed, you have fixed ideas as to what you should get from your wife and children. You may have a romantic affair outside marriage but will not tolerate such behaviour on the part of your wife. In this matter you are very suspicious of her.

AN AUGUST WIFE:

You are a loveable person and by your grace, dignity and social nature you attract many people. You can manage your house very efficiently and you are a right wife for an energetic and enthusiastic husband. You are patient and make sacrifices. You pay every attention to the welfare of your husband and children. Only you know what sacrifice you make for them but others hardly understand your devotion. You are very passionate and need a virile and masculine husband to satisfy your romantic nature.

Lucky Days

Sundays, Mondays and Thursdays are your lucky days and

you should try to take your important move on these days.

Lucky Colours

Your lucky colours are golden, yellow, orange and purple. It is suggested that you make use of these colours either in your clothes or at home.

Lucky Jewels And Stones

You should use ruby, topaz or amber as your lucky jewels and stones.

Before selecting your lucky jewels, colours and days please refer to your individual numbers and find out the common factor and select the final jewel or colour.

BORN IN SEPTEMBER

The month of September is dominated by the planet Mercury and, therefore, you are governed by Mercurian characteristics.

Character

You are very active and quick. This is true not only of your physical agility but also of your mind. You are very skillful and have intuition. You are proficient in games where you use your hands as well as your brain. You have the capacity to judge the ability of your opponents in games and know very well how to take advantage of the weak points of your opponents. You are fond of oratory and eloquence in expressing yourself. You are energetic and constantly working. You are adroit and crafty and a constant schemer. You have the capacity to pursue your objective and know very well how to plan to achieve your aims. You hardly lose any opportunity and put every hour to use. You are deeply interested in occult subjects and would like to master all the intricacies of abstruse subjects. You are a lover of nature and are fond of animals like horses and dogs. You are also interested in reading books on scientific subjects; romantic subjects are of little interest to you.

Health

Your basic health defect is biliousness and nervousness. Your biliousness is closely related to your psychological disturbances. Experience shows that your biliousness increases with increase in tension and is reduced or disappears when your nervous trouble is under control. If you suffer from this trouble, you may have paralytic trouble, mostly in your arms or upper portion. You may also experience stammering or impediments in speech.

Marriage And Friends

Your most harmonious relationship is with those who are born between 21st August to 20th September, between 21st January and 20th February and between 21st April to 20th May. You also have a natural attraction towards people born on the 5th, 14th and 23rd of any month. It is, therefore, advisable that you select your life partner or friends from this period.

A SEPTEMBER HUSBAND:

You are a lucky and successful husband. Your selection is good and usually you select a person of your own type. You love your partner. You expect neatness and cleanliness from your wife and also desire that she should share with you the joys of life. You want her to be stylish and full of fire and life. You also love your children and love home life.

A SEPTEMBER WIFE:

You will make a wonderful wife for an enthusiastic husband. You are a witty and clever conversationalist with a wonderful social presence. You will assist your husband in his business. You may also start your own activity and add to the family income. You will be happy if married to a passionate and possessive man.

You have interest in the home as well as outside. You have many activities and manage them well. You like tidiness and though you seldom do your own work, you get it done by your commanding personality.

Lucky Days

Your lucky days are Wednesdays, Fridays and Saturdays and you should try to take all your important decisions on these days.

Lucky Colours

Your lucky colours are green and white. You should, therefore, try to wear clothes of these colours and paint your house in these colours.

Lucky Jewels And Stones

The most lucky jewels for you are sapphire, emerald and diamond.

Before selecting your lucky jewels, colours and days, please refer to your individual number and find out a common factor and make the final selection.

BORN IN OCTOBER

The month of October is ruled by the planet Venus. You are therefore governed by Venusian characteristics.

Character

You have a pleasant personality. Your presence radiates enthusiasm, energy and charm. Sometimes others may be required to put aside their ideas of morality and social conduct in understanding and appreciating your feelings and views. You are gifted with health, vitality and warmth. You have a great attraction for beauty and love. You desire a life full of ease, luxury, money and happiness. You prefer spending to saving. It is true that you have vigour and warmth of passions but it does not necessarily mean that you are fond of sex. You are a born artist and art and beauty in life have an attraction for you. Therefore your love for nature and beauty should not be misunderstood. You try to understand the grievances and difficulties of others through a considerate approach. You prefer joy to gloom and have the capacity to carry others along with you to moments of enjoyment. Your outlook is bright and vivacious. You like to remain honest and truthful in love and friendship.

Health

On the whole you have good health. However, you are susceptible to fever and impurities of blood and nervousness. You may also suffer from pain in the back and severe headache and peculiar maladies of the skin.

Marriage And Friends

You will find lasting union and friendship with persons born between 21st September and 20th October, between 21st January and 20th February and between 21st May and 20th June. You also have a natural attraction for those born on the 6th, 15th and 24th of any month.

AN OCTOBER HUSBAND:

You like marriage and usually marry early in life. You expect your partner to be neat and have charm and grace. Yours is usually a large family. You are very kind, generous and devoted and love your children and home. Though you create a lively atmosphere in the home, you somehow find it difficult to provide all the necessities of the members of the family. This may sometimes create unpleasantness.

AN OCTOBER WIFE:

You are a devoted mother and a loving wife, satisfied with your husband's efforts on your behalf. You love domestic life and are a perfect home maker. You never resort to divorce and would rather induce extreme hardship than desert your husband. You have the tact to get along with people and to attract an interesting social circle. At the same time you never neglect your home duties. Though you are attractive and have a group of admirers seeking your favour, you are sober and never encourage indiscriminate flirtation.

Lucky Days

Your lucky days are Mondays, Tuesdays, Thursdays and Fridays. You should therefore take your important decisions and actions on these days.

Lucky Colours

You should wear blue, rose and pink colours or use these colours for painting the walls of your house.

Lucky Jewels And Stones

Opal and pearl are lucky for you and you should use them for good luck.

Before selecting your lucky jewels, colours and days, please refer to your individual number and fined out a common factor and make the final selection.

BORN IN NOVEMBER

The planet Mars rules the month of November and therefore you are governed by Martian characteristics.

Character

You are a fighter and a soldier. You are aggressive and will not stop till you achieve your aim. You have the capacity to fight against adverse elements and circumstances. You are also a fighter in your mental world. You are very active, brisk and energetic. You cannot be tactful or delicate in your talk but your intentions are always good. Your vigorous manner should not be misconstrued as rough behaviour. You are fiery and dashing and do not have sickly sentiments. You are a brave person to whom conflict does not bring the thought of danger. You are exceedingly devoted to your friends and will fight for them. You are very generous and magnanimous. You have sympathy and consideration for the weak. You love children and animals. Your main characteristics are aggression, resistance, courage, enthusiasm and quickness.

Health

Your main health defect arises from heat and you are susceptible to piles, fevers, small pox etc. You are also likely to suffer from kidney or bladder trouble. Throat trouble, bronchitis and laryngitis also often pester you

Marriage And Friends

You will find a lasting union or friendship with those born between 21st October and 20th November, between 19th

February and 20th March and between 21st June and 20th July. You also have a natural attraction towards persons born on the 9th, 18th and 27th of any month. You should, therefore, find your life partners and friend from this period.

A NOVEMBER HUSBAND:

You have vigour and strength and are very passionate and enthusiastic about married life. You are fond of a beautiful wife and like her to be submissive and passive to your sexual desires. You are fond of your family and children and like to have a good house. You usually lead a good married life in spite of your hot tempered nature and eccentricities. You have a romantic mental picture of what you want in your wife. This mental picture demands perfection. You desire a clever and very good wife. The most difficult thing for your wife is to satisfy your romantic conception of physical love.

A NOVEMBER WIFE:

You make a wonderful wife for an ambitious man. You are witty and a clever conversationalist with a wonderful social presence. You can assist your husband in his business. You may also start your own activity and add to family income. You will be happy if married to a passionate and possessive man. Though you like your children, you are not very much attached to them and like them to develop on their own. You must always keep yourself busy, otherwise your moodiness will disturb your family life. It is advisable that you have a friend in whom you can confide.

Lucky Days

Mondays, Tuesdays, Thursdays and Fridays are your lucky days and you should take all your important decisions and actions on these days.

Lucky Colours

Red, white and yellow are your lucky colours and you should try to use them in your clothes and in your house.

Lucky Jewels And Stones

Your lucky jewels are coral or pearl and you should use them for obtaining success in life.

Before selecting your lucky jewels, colours and days, please refer to your individual number and find out the common factor and make the final selection.

BORN IN DECEMBER

The month of December is governed by the planet Jupiter. You are therefore dominated by Jupiterian characteristics.

Character

Jupiter stands for morality, pure love and justice and is known as the greatest benefactor. You are therefore devotional, religious and have dignity. You are generally lucky and prosperous. You are confident and self-reliant and take your own decisions. You are fond of show and like to observe form, order and law. You are jovial in spirit and cordial in manner. Your passions are healthy, spontaneous and without inhibitions. You are free in your expressions. You take an active interest in sports and outdoor activities from your earliest youth. You have tremendous enthusiasm in life. You are not at all self-centered. Your intellect is of a very high order, your nature for sighted and practical. You have a kind of vision that understands the world and love it for what it is and not for what it ought to be. You are a broad minded person, tolerant, humorous and truthful. You are open hearted with good understanding and are entirely lacking in malice or petty jealousies.

If you possess in excess the qualities of Jupiter, you have arrogance, boastfulness, vindictiveness, criminal jealousy, tyranny and superstition. You are also egoistic, selfish and shrewd.

Your basic characteristics are ambition, leadership, religion, pride, honour, love for nature and enthusiasm.

Health

Your main health defects relate to blood circulation, the arterial system and the liver. You are likely to suffer from chest and lung disorders, throat afflictions, gout and sudden fevers. You may also suffer from tonsilitis, sore throat, diphtheria, adenoids, pneumonia and pleurisy. You are also likely to suffer from skin diseases.

Marriage And Friends

Your most harmonious relationship is with those who are born between 21st November and 20th December, between 21st March and 20th April and between 21st July and 20th August. You also have attraction towards those who are born on the 3rd, 12th, 21st and 30th of any month. You should therefore select your partner and friends from these periods.

A DECEMBER HUSBAND:

As a general rule you attain puberty at an early age and marry early. However, as you are ambitious, your ambition makes you expect too many things from your wife which results in disappointment. You desire to have a wife whom you can be proud of. She should have an attractive personality, commanding presence, charming manners, and intelligence. You are most loving, thoughtful and considerate. Your passions are adventures and demand immediate satisfaction.

A DECEMBER WIFE:

You are the best companion to your husband. You are not an intruder but take an active interest in the business of your husband. You are efficient in house-keeping and have a sympathetic and balanced attitude towards your children. Your passions are healthy and joyous and your approach to physical love is highly refined and inspiring.

Lucky Days

Your lucky days are Tuesdays, Thursdays and Fridays.

Lucky Colours

Your lucky colours are yellow, violet, purple and green. You should use these colours either in your clothes or at home.

Lucky Jewels And Stones

Your lucky jewels are topaz and amethyst.

Before selecting your lucky jewels, colours and days, please refer to your individual number and find out the common factor and select the final jewel or the colours etc.

SUMMARY CHART OF THE MONTHS

Month	*Characteristics*	*Health Problems*	*Marriage Partner and Friends born between*	*Lucky Days*	*Lucky Colours*	*Lucky Jewels*
January	Septic, slow, decisive, cautious, Analytical, Methodical	Nervousness, Melancholia Rheumatism Biliousness	21st Dec. to 20th Jan. 21st April to 20th May 21st Aug. to 20th Sept. Nos. 8, 17, 26	Wednesday Thursday Friday	Grey, Violet, Purple, Black	Pearl, Moonstone Garnet, Sapphire
February	Honour, Prestige, Dignity, Sensitivity, Good advisor	Poor blood circulation, Heart, Bladder, Kidney	21st Jan. to 20th Feb. 21st May to 20th June 21st Sep. to 20th Oct. Nos. 8, 17, 26	Wednesday Thursday Saturday	Grey, Violet, Purple	Topaz, Amethyst Diamond
March	Courageous, Generous, Dual personality	Depression, Insomnia, Rheumatism	19th feb. to 20th Mar. 21st June to 20th July 21st Oct. to 20th Nov. Nos. 3, 12, 21, 30	Tuesday Thursday Friday	Yelllow, Violet, Purple, Green	Topaz, Emerald Sapphire

April	Dominating, Energetic, Hot-tempered, Active, Organiser, Obstinate	Fever, Inflammability, Teeth, Ears, Eyes	21st Mar. to 20th April 21st July to 20th Aug. 21st Nov. to 20th Dec. Nos. 9, 18, 27	Monday Tuesday Thursday Friday	Rose, Crimson, Pink	Pearl, Garnet, Coral
May	Generosity, Sacrifice, Endurance, Law of travel and Picnic	Respiratory track, Kidney	21st Apr. to 20th May 21st Aug. to 20th Sept. 21st Dec. to 20th Jan. Nos. 6, 15, 24	Monday Tuesday Thursday Friday	Blue, Rose, Pink	Emerald, Pearl, Diamond
June	Sharp, Brilliant, Quick, Moody	Psychological, Nervousness, Blood disorders	21st May to 20th June 21st Sept. to 20th Oct. 21st Jan. to 20th Feb. Nos. 5, 14, 23	Tuesday Thursday Friday	Yellow, Violet, Purple, Green	Sapphire, Emerald
July	Industrious, Speculative, Sensitive, Moody, Musician	Gastri trouble, Rheumatism, Respiratory track	21st June to 20th July 21st Oct. to 20th Nov. 21st Feb. to 20th Mar. Nos. 2, 11, 20, 29	Sunday Monday Wednesday Thursday	Green, Yellow	Pearl, Diamond

August	Originality, Dignity, Talents, Style, Grace	Heart, Eye sight, Over exertion	21st July to 20th Aug. 21st Nov. to 20th Dec. 21st Mar. to 20th Apr. Nos. 1, 10, 19, 28	Sunday Monday Thursday	Gold, Yellow, Orange, Purple	Topaz, Amber.
September	Activity, Quickness, Skill, Intuition, Oratory	Biliousness, Nervolusness	21st Aug. to 20th Sept. 21st Dec. to 20th Jan. 21st Apr. to 20th May Nos. 5, 14, 23	Wednesday Friday Sunday	Green, White	Emerald Diamond, Sapphire.
October	Enthusiasm, Energy, Charm, Spendthrift	Fever, Impurities of blood, skin	21st Sept. to 20th Oct. 21st Jan. to 20th feb. 21st May to 20th June Nos. 6, 15, 24	Monday Tuesday Thursday	Blue, Rose, Pink	Opal, Pearl.
November	Fighter, Active, Brisk, Dashing, Courageous	Fever, Piles, Kidney, Bladder, Throat	21st Oct. to 20th Nov. 21st Feb. to 20th Mar. 21st June to 20th July Nos. 9, 18, 27	Monday Tuesday Thursday Friday	Red White, Yellow	Coral Pearl.
December	Religion, Morality, Love, Justice	Poor blood circulation, Artetrial system, Liver	21st Nov. to 20th Dec. 21st Mar. to 20th Apr. 21st July to 20th Aug. Nos. 3, 12, 21, 30	Tuesday Thursday Friday	Yellow, Violet, Purple, Green	Topaz, Amethyst.

CHAPTER 14

FULL SIGNIFICANCE OF YOUR BIRTH-DATE

After discussing the date of the month and the month of birth, I shall elucidate further details about the birth-date as a whole.

Let us suppose that your complete date of birth is 7th May 1961. This birth-date has been selected just at random. In any birth-date we have to take three factors into consideration. The first is the date of the month which, in this case, is the 7th; the second is the month, which is May; and the third is the total of all the numbers in the birth-date which, in the present case, is:

7 + 5 + 1 + 9 + 6 + 1 = 29 = 2.

The Date Of The Month

We have already discussed and studied the significance of this date in Chapter 10. The date of birth is the individual seal depicting the basic characteristics of the individual. This date also shows the important years in your life and helps you to improve your personality by repeating its frequency, in day-to-day action. Being born on the 7th of the month, you have originality, individuality and independence. You love to travel and are like a free bird. This is a spiritual number and Supreme Consciousness is developed in you. Your behaviour is a mystery to others and you are often absent-minded. Your important and lucky years in life are 7, 16, 25, 34, 43, 52 and 61 etc.

The Month Of Birth

The month of birth shows your social circle. It shows your childhood and also the social status of your family. It also indicates the influence of brothers, sisters and playmates. It shows your attraction towards friends and relatives who are governed by the characteristics shown by the number of the month. In the present case the month is May i.e. the fifth month. Therefore your social circle is dominated by number five and the planet Mercury. You are, therefore, attracted towards those who are intelligent, industrious and have quickness, scientific pursuits, business abilities and intuition. You select friends who are well read and can impart their knowledge. You do not like to talk about ordinary things in life and dislike "kitchen" discussions. The month of May is also dominated by the planet Venus. You are therefore also attracted to friends who are governed by Venusian qualities such as art and beauty.

The Total Of The Birth-Date

The gross total of the complete birth-date indicates the number of destiny also called the Fadic Number. In the present case, it is two. It shows your personality in a general way. Since the number two is governed by the planet Moon, you are unsteady in life, whimsical and changing. Your individual date is seven which is governed by the planet Neptune which also has similar characteristics. Therefore, you are more dominated by the Moon and your ideas, behaviour, likes, dislikes etc. are heightened. Your important years in life will be 2, 11, 20, 29, 38, 47, 56, 65 etc. where the total of the digits, when reduced to a single digit, comes to two. This destiny number is not necessarily a lucky number and it shows both good and bad events in life. Thus, there is a difference between the date of the month, which is called the Ruling

Number, and the Destiny or Fadic Number. Please refer to your individual Fadic Number explained at the end of each Ruling Number from 1 to 9.

Thus, from the complete birth-date, you know your characteristics in detail as derived from your Ruling Number, from the month of birth and also from the Fadic Number.

I shall now proceed further to unravel your additional angularities from your birth date.

Numerical Horoscope

You can arrange the date of birth in the form of a horoscope. From this horoscope you can know the level of the thought, whether you think on an idealistic plane or on a material plane or on a lower plane. You can describe it in the form of Dharma, Artha and Karma or Satwa, Rajas and Tamas. Let us suppose that your complete date of birth is 12-6-1853.

I now give below a standard form of the numerical horoscope

3	1	9	Dharma,	Satwa
6	7	5	Artha,	Rajas
2	8	4	Karma,	Tamas

You have now to place the numbers in your given birth-date in the appropriate squares allotted to each number in the standard horoscope. Your birth date is 12-6-1853. While placing the numbers you do not have to consider the number of the century. The year of the birth is 1953.

Here we have to omit 19 and consider only the year 53. The horoscope of the birth date 12-6-53 will be as under:

3	1	
6	5	
2		

On the mental level he is dominated by number 3 and 1. The number 3 is governed by the planet Jupiter and the number 1 is ruled by the Sun. It means that the mental make-up of the person is dominated by the characteristics of Jupiter and the Sun and the person is ambitious, religious and dignified. The Sun gives him originality, oratory and activity.

On the material level, he has the qualities of Venus and Mercury. Mercury is a business planet and Venus shows art. The combination produces a person who will use his creative art or talent to earn money.

On the lower plane, the person is governed by the imaginative faculty of the Moon. But his imagination will be on the level of Karma only and he may utilise his success for indulging in lower vices only. We can summarise the character of the person and say that he has art and creativity shown by the number 6 and the planet Venus; he has originality and activity shown by the number 1 and the planet Sun; he also has ambition shown by number 3 and the planet Jupiter and he will utilise all these qualities to make money and obtain success in practical life as shown by the number 5 and the planet Mercury. The Moon indicates that he may indulge in low vices.

If in a birth-date a number is repeated a second time or a

third time, that number gets double or triple power. If in the above birth-date, the month is January instead of June, in the horoscope number 1 will be repeated a second time. If the year of birth is 51 instead of 53, the number one will be repeated for the third time (12-1-1951). If the birth date is 16-6-1953, the number 6 is repeated two times; that means the influence of Venus is doubled. In such a case we have to add a line to the number to show its double power, add two lines to show the triple power. Thus, the birth date 12-1-1951 will have the following horoscope.

	1''	
	5	
2		

In the above case, the triple power of the number 1 is indicated by the additional two lines.

Missing Numbers

After preparing the necessary horoscope from any known birth date, we may notice that certain numbers are missing in the horoscope. According to an age old theory, the missing numbers indicate the effect of our Karma (action) in our previous birth. Due to certain acts of ours in our previous birth, we have to suffer the disadvantages of the missing numbers. We will not get the benefits of the planets which are missing in the horoscope. For instance, the number 3 is missing in the horoscope; this means that the person does not have characteristics such as ambition, love of religion, prestige, honour, dignity etc. which are indicated by the planet Jupiter. Supposing the number 8 represented by the planet Saturn is missing, the person lacks a practical outlook and materialistic philosophy shown by the planet Saturn. In short, the missing numbers indicate a lack of power represented by the missing numbers. It is, therefore, advisable that the person should understand his virtues as well as his drawbacks and limitations and try to develop the qualities of the missing numbers which would help him overcome the obstacles in life and lead a successful life.

Conjunction of Planets

When two numbers are in adjacent squares, they are in conjunction with each other. In that case the effects are combined. In one of the horoscopes above, there is a conjunction of 3 and 6; 6 and 2.

According to the Indian grantha (book) "Yantra Chintamani", every planet has its "Yantra" (Talisman), which is to be prepared either from gold or silver or copper. You have to worship this Yantra with appropriate Mantra of that planet and as per the number of repetitions prescribed for that Mantra. You can also use it as a talisman and wear it on the neck or in a ring. This will help you gain good health, wealth and riches.

The various Talismen are as under:

1 TALISMAN OF THE SUN: NUMBER 1

Sun

If your Ruling Number is 1, i.e. if you are born on the 1st, 10th, 19th or 28th of any month, you can use this talisman for your prosperity. Your Ruling Number 1 is placed in the centre at the top line and the total of the square in any direction is fifteen. You should make this Yantra (Talisman) engraved on a plate or a ring made of gold. If you make a ring, then wear it on the ring finger which is also known as the finger of Sun.

2 TALISMAN OF THE MOON: NUMBER 2

If your Ruling Number is 2, i.e. if you are born on the 2nd, 11th, 20th or 29th of any month, you can use this talisman for your prosperity. Your Ruling number 2 is placed in the centre at the top line and the total of the square in any direction is eighteen. You should get this Yantra engraved on a plate or a ring made of silver. If you make a ring, then wear it on the fourth finger.

3 TALISMAN OF THE JUPITER: NUMBER 3

If your Ruling Number is 3, i.e., if you are born on the 3rd, 12th, 21st or 30th of any month, you can use this talisman for your prosperity. The total of the squares in any direction is twenty-seven. You should get this Yantra engraved on a plate or a ring made of gold. If you make a ring, then wear it on the ring finger or the first finger which is also known as the Jupiter finger.

4 TALISMAN OF THE URANUS: NUMBER 4

If your Ruling Number is 4, i.e., if you are born on the

Uranus

4th, 13th, 22nd or 31st of any month, you can use this talisman for your prosperity. The total of the square in any direction is thirty-six. You should get this Yantra engraved on a plate or a ring made of tin metal. If you make a ring, then wear it on the fourth finger.

5 TALISMAN OF THE MERCURY: NUMBER 5

Mercury

If your Ruling Number is 5, i.e., if you are born on the 5th, 14th or 23rd of any month, you can use this talisman for your prosperity. The total of the squares in any direction is twenty four. You should get this Yantra engraved on a plate or a ring made of brass. If you make a ring, then wear it on the fourth finger which is also known as the Mercury finger.

6 TALISMAN OF THE VENUS: NUMBER 6

Venus

If your Ruling Number is 6, i.e., if you are born on the 6th, 15th or 24th of any month, you can use this talisman for your prosperity. Your Ruling Number is placed in the centre at the top line and the total of the square in any direction is thirty. You should get this Yantra engraved on a plate or a ring made of silver. If you make a ring, then wear it on the ring finger.

7 TALISMAN OF THE NEPTUNE: NUMBER 7

Naptune

If your Ruling Number is 7, i.e., if you are born on the 7th, 16th or 25th of any month, you can use this talisman for your prosperity. The total of the squares in any direction is thirty-nine. You should get this Yantra engraved on a plate or a ring made of gold. If you make a ring, then wear it on the ring finger.

8 TALISMAN OF THE SATURN: NUMBER 8

Saturn

If your Ruling Number is 8, i.e., if you are born on the 8th, 17th or 26th of any month, you can use this talisman for your prosperity. The total of the squares in any direction is thirty-three. You should get this Yantra engraved on a plate or a ring made of zinc. If you make a ring, then wear it on second finger which is known as the Saturn finger.

9 TALISMAN OF THE MARS: NUMBER 9

Mars

If your Ruling Number is 9, i.e., if you are born on the 9th, 18th or 27th of any month, you can use this talisman for your prosperity. The total of the squares in any direction is twenty-one. You should get this Yantra engraved on a plate or a ring made of copper. If you make a ring, wear it on the ring finger.

Your Birth Year Cycle

According to the theory of numerology the year of birth is also important in some respects. There is always rise and fall in life and this rise or fall takes place at a certain interval in life. In order to find out the year of change you have to add the total of the digits shown in the year of birth only. Supposing you are born in the year 1954, you add up all the numbers in this year, the total of which comes to 19. You have to add this 19 to the year of birth which is 1954. The total therefore is 1973. This year of 1973 is important in some respects and shows a change in life, either a rise or a fall. You can find out the years of change in the following manner:

The year of birth	1954
Add: The total of digits	19
The first period of change	1973
Add: The total of the year	20
The second period of change	1993

You have to continue adding the total of the year thus arrived every time and find out the year of change.

An example explaining your complete birth-date

Uptil now we have studied the various aspects of the ruling number of the month, of the complete total of the date of the birth and the total of year only. In addition to this we have also studied in chapter 2 influence of numbers and Rasis (Zodiacs) on the human body, division of Rasis into four Elements, Square of affinity. We shall now take the birth date and solve or explain it in the above perspective. Let us suppose that your birth date is 12-6-1949.

1. Since your birth date is 12, the ruling number is 3.

You are therefore governed by the Jupiterian characteristics which are ambition, honour, dignity, prestige etc.

2. Your important years in life are 3, 12, 21, 30, 39, 48, 57, 66, etc.
3. Your lucky dates are Tuesdays, Thursdays and Fridays and lucky colours are yellow, violet, purple and green. Your lucky stones are topaz, cat's eye and amethyst.
4. You are born in the month of June which is dominated by the planet Mercury and also Venus. The month indicates your social circle and friends or relatives to whom you are attracted. You are, therefore, likely to be in the company of people who are intelligent, businesslike, practical and also of artistic qualities.
5. In order to find out the Fadic Number, you have to add the total of your complete birth date which in this case is 32 with the single digit as 5. So you are also dominated by number 5 and the Mercurian qualities. All the years of age where the final total is 5 are also important in your life, either for good or for bad.
6. The year of birth is 1949 and as seen in this chapter only we have to find out the important years by adding the total of birth year to the birth year. We have again to add the total of the year thus arrived to the respective year and so on. In your case, therefore, the total of birth year 1949 is 23 which when added comes to 1972 which is an important year.
7. Since you are born in the period 21st May to 20th June, you are dominated by the Rasi Mithuna (Gemini)

which has dominance on shoulders.

8. The above period is under the element air and therefore you run the danger of falling from high places.
9. Square of affinity—You have a natural affinity to those who are born in September, December, March and June of any year.
10. Numerical horoscope.—We can also prepare a numerical horoscope from your above date and describe your qualities according to the method studied in this chapter only.

This is how from your birth-date, we can describe your various characteristics, likes and dislikes, your health, finance, marriage partner, etc. etc.

CHAPTER 15

YOUR LUCKY NUMBER AND MONEY NUMBER

Lucky Number

By knowing your lucky number, financial activities can often be arranged in the hour on any particular day that corresponds to your lucky number and thus greater benefit can be derived than would be otherwise possible.

In order to find out the lucky number, you have to know the day of the week on which you were born. You have to know also the hour of the day on which you were born. The exact minute of the hour does not matter much. In the table given below the hours of each day from Sunday to Saturday, a.m. and p.m. are given, together with the number that rules the hour. The number shown for your day and hour of birth will be your lucky number.

In the table given, some numbers are in bold type and others in ordinary type. Those in bold type show the positive hours and those in ordinary type, negative hours. Positive hours strengthen the fortunate vibrations and will bring greater luck than the negative hours. Whatever hour you are born in, positive or negative, the number ruling that hour will be your lucky number. Once you ascertain your lucky number, from the chart you can see the hours on the various days of the week when your number is exercising power.

You are now requested to refer to the table given on page 133. In this table you will find your lucky number with the following example. If you were born on a Monday between

Birth Time	SUN		MON		TUE		WED		THU		FRI		SAT	
	A.M.	P.M.	A.M.	P.M.	A.M.	P.M.	A.M.	P.M.	A.M.	P.M.	A.M.	P.M.	A.M.	P.M.
0-1	1	3	7	6	9	8	5	1	3	7	6	9	8	5
1-2	6	9	8	5	4	3	2	6	9	8	5	4	3	2
2-3	5	1	3	7	6	9	8	5	1	3	7	6	9	8
3-4	2	6	9	8	5	4	3	2	6	9	8	5	4	3
4-5	8	5	1	3	7	6	9	8	5	1	3	7	6	9
5-6	3	2	6	9	8	5	4	3	2	6	9	8	5	4
6-7	9	8	5	1	3	7	6	9	8	5	1	3	7	6
7-8	4	3	2	6	9	8	5	4	3	2	6	9	8	5
8-9	6	9	8	5	1	3	7	6	9	8	5	1	3	7
9-10	5	4	3	2	6	9	8	5	4	3	2	6	9	8
10-11	7	6	9	8	5	1	3	7	6	9	8	5	1	3
11-12	8	5	4	3	2	6	9	8	5	4	3	2	6	9

6 and 7 a.m. your lucky number would be 5 and the hours on any other day governed by the number 5 could be used for furthering specific activities particularly if you could use those hours when a positive 5 is exercising power.

This positive hour or hours would be best for any thing of an active or constructive nature, but the negative hour ruled by your lucky number would be extremely favourable for studies, research, investigation etc., and could be used for concentrating upon the result of a horse race; because during these negative hours the power of inspiration would be considerably stronger than during the positive hours which are more for active interests.

Money Number

In order to know your money number, you have to write your full name i.e. your name, your father's name and your surname. The numbers for each name should be set out separately, then the total of each name added and the final result reduced to 22, or under, should it be above 22. In case of ladies who are married they should put husband's name in place of father's name. While allotting the numbers to each alphabet please refer to the next chapter (What's in a name?). Once the final number of your name has been obtained, the planetary or zodiacal vibration associated with the number will give the overall indication regarding the general financial fortunes of life.

Let us take an illustration. Let us suppose that your name is as under:

YASHODHAN	ASHOK	GOKHALE
1 1 3 5 7 4 5 1 5	1 3 5 7 2	3 7 2 5 1 3 5
32	18	26
5	9	8

The three totals are added: 5 + 9 + 8 = 22. All the attributes of the numbers from 1 to 22 are given in the following pages of this chapter. In the above case since the number is 22 please refer to that number at the end. This system is based on the interpretations given according to the Tarot System.

The number ONE in its influence over your money interests shows that money will be earned and derived from quite a variety of sources. Some of these can be of an intellectual and mental nature and others can be connected with travel, transport and certain mechanical affairs, for the influence gives quite a degree of adaptability and it will not take you long to see the possibilities latent in any given condition, to acquire a sufficiency of knowledge to handle it and then to turn it to practical use. Yet, you will need to see that you do not fritter away and gain that occurs, or any reserve that you create during the progressive periods, by certain forms of irresponsible or thoughtless expenditure. Particular care will always be required in the making of financial agreements and arrangements and in the signing of financial papers. Never take things too much for granted.

The number TWO causes you to have a strong sense of thrift without necessarily being mean. You will not mind spending money, within reason, but you will always do your utmost to obtain full value for the money you do spend. You will invariably do your best to regulate both income and expenditure and this will apply to private as well as to business activities. You will benefit through constructive developments to do with either work or business and through proper attention to details, but there will be occasions when it will be wiser not to express undue criticism of the decisions or actions of others who may be associated with your financial interests, for this would only tend to create misunderstanding and unpleasantness and could disturb co-operation or any form of partnership. Additional income could be obtained by using literary ability (if you do not already use this professionally), and by obtaining knowledge of such things as accountancy, costing etc. and using this knowledge in a part time capacity. Sometimes, interests to do with food analysis and research and methods of distribution can be made to step up normal income.

The number THREE signifies, in a rather peculiar manner, that you will either gravitate more or less automatically towards interests connected with the financial side of life or they will be drawn to you without any necessarily voluntary action on your part. In either event the use that you make of the opportunities brought by this contact will decide the degree of financial benefit that you ultimately derive. You will have a strong desire for the luxuries and amenities of life but will want money to come easily and without undue personal effort. If this tendency is given way to, there will be a danger of yielding to temptations that come into your life and that are brought either by circumstances or by unscrupulous individuals who make suggestions that whilst being attractive are not strictly honest, and if given way to, could involve you in transactions of a fraudulent character. Your main weakness will be a reliance upon others, but though this can aid you in obtaining money, it will not bring permanent security unless you have a partner or someone to cooperate with, who is strictly honest and straightforward.

The number FOUR shows you have the ability to work hard and long in order to obtain money, and with effort you can command quite a good income irrespective of whether you work for yourself or for others. At the same time you will always need to watch expenditure for you will always have an urge to spend money, and unless this is properly controlled you will find yourself taking up obligations and liabilities that will not always be easily redeemed; rather they can produce temporary embarrassment. You are not necessarily personally extravagant, but it will be extremely difficult to retrain from spending money on equipment and machinery, especially if you work for yourself, in order to bring about greater efficiency. You will also want certain of the amenities that help to make domestic life more agreeable, but in obtaining these will once again need to use discrimination so as not to overload yourself with payments out. In speculation, forethought will be required and undue, risks should not be taken, but you will have quite shrewd judgement regarding investments.

The number FIVE is an exceptionally fortunate number to have as ruler over your financial affairs and shows that you will derive many financial benefits during the course of your life and will experience quite a deal of financial luck and good fortune. Benefit will come through your work and vocational interests, through speculation and investment and quite possibly through legacy or inheritance as well. At the same time there will be occasions when extravagant inclinations will need to be resisted and when unwise risks to do with speculation or investment should be avoided, for should these inclinations be given way to, then temporary periods of loss and of financial embarrassment can occur. A great deal will, therefore, depend upon your own handling of affairs. A common sense approach to all financial matters will ensure progress and a building up of a very substantial reserve, but a taking of affairs too much for granted can interfere with progress and, as stated, bring losses.

The number SIX exercises quite a helpful influence over money interests. It creates a vibration of attraction whereby money will come to you, sometimes with, but little effort on your part. This does not imply that you should take things too easily and expect circumstances or luck to bring you everything you desire because if you do so you can be sadly mistaken. If, however, proper personal effort is put forth then the fortunate vibration inherent in this planet will help to bring many benefits, both through work and business, and from time to time through speculation and investment. You will also gain through the cooperation of others and through constructive partnership and marriage, provided that a wise choice of marriage partner has been made. On the other hand, should an unwise choice of marriage or business partner have occurred, then the danger of loss will be intensified.

The number SEVEN signifies that from a general stand point money matters will be reasonably progressive and there will be periods of luck and good fortune. Money and income can be derived through a blending of a variety of activities and by combining your main vocational interests with others of a secondary character.

Fluctuations will occur both of income and expenditure and in the latter direction you will need to exercise a degree of common sense and not rely unduly upon the factor of good luck, for though there will be fortunate periods, you can also experience losses and setbacks by taking certain things too much for granted. On occasions you will benefit through speculation and, in fact, there can be some attraction towards the taking of a risk in the hope of obtaining a substantial gain. You will, however, need to see that this attraction does not become too strong for sometimes your "hunches" will be wrong, and if you take unwise risks then, the resulting loss can cause you considerable strain and anxiety and interfere with your progress in other directions of vocational nature.

The number EIGHT shows that the factor of ambition

will be very marked in your life where money is concerned. You will want money both from the stand point of the security it can give when you have built up a good reserve, as you will invariably do your best to do, and as a means to buy yourself as many of the things you desire, irrespective of whether these are of a domestic or a business nature, or both.

You will always try to regulate expenditure, and on occasions may need to fight against a sense of undue caution which, if allowed to go to an extreme, could stop you from spending money even when it is necessary to do so. From a normal stand point, however, it will be the practical side of your nature which will regulate your activities, showing that you can be careful and yet not necessarily deny yourself of either the necessities or of some of the luxuries of life. You will gain through a developing of business activities and by the holding of responsibilities which link the business and financial sides of life with those of a social, public and political nature, and where you can use your power of organisation.

The number NINE indicates that many of your personal hopes and wishes will be associated with money and with the financial side of life. Alternatively, the obtaining of money and a good income will enable you to bring about a realising of other hopes and wishes connected with the social and public sides of life and with affectional and friendly matters.

Normally, the number will give much forethought and a deal of practicality in the handling of financial affairs and will strengthen your sense of responsibility in that direction. You will be likely at times during your life to hold positions of trust where other people's money is involved. But you should always make a point of seeing that this money never becomes mixed with your own for this could produce some misunderstanding and even loss, in the future. You will benefit more as a result of constructive investment than by the taking of speculative risks, for your judgement on the former will be far better than that with the latter.

The number TEN signifies that you will have sudden gains and sudden losses, some of which will be caused through unexpected alteration of your vocational activities and others through speculation or the taking of risks. If, however, your originality of thought and action aid you, you can derive more gain than loss, particularly if you do your best to plan out affairs ahead and to take proper account of the possible risks and snags that can occur. You will need to watch matters to do with the affections or any form of business partnership or cooperation, for any sudden upset or misunderstanding will react adversely and bring a danger of loss. Maintaining of cooperation will be essential. The number does show a great possibility of gain through such things as sweepstakes, lotteries and football pools.

The number ELEVEN exerts a rather peculiar influence. It gives you the ability to take a long term view of affairs, to correctly appraise future possibilities and to use your power of suggestion to influence other people with whom you have financial dealings so that they come round to your line of thought and action and are willing to assist and help you. On the other hand, you will always need to guard against trouble or loss through the deception or trickery of others, and at times through dishonesty, actual theft or burglary. There will be occasions when as a result of encountering difficulties, you will be tempted to do things to overcome the difficulties, that at more normal times would not be contemplated. These temptations should be resisted.

The number TWELVE indicates that although there will be an experiencing of fluctuations in connection with money matters, from both the income and expenditure stand points, there will be periods of luck and good fortune as well as a safeguarding of the main financial interests of your life. At the same time it will not be wise to take things too much for granted or to become careless in the handling of money matters as opportunities for deriving benefit could be lost on the one hand and these could be an experiencing of difficulties on the other hand through a neglect of practical safeguards. Benefit will be derived through a creating of good will and by a proper cultivation of friendly associations as well as through contact with interests of philosophical, psychic and kindred nature, but there can be loss as a result of imposition, deception and false friends, and through acting too literally upon the suggestions and advice of other people. The inclination to make money easily or quickly should always be resisted, for if this is given way to, it can bring contact with dubious characters or a doing of things that strictly speaking are not straight forward.

The number THIRTEEN signifies that you will not find it easy to resist the urge to spend money. If this urge is given in to, it will cause you to be extravagant and hence will bring times when your expenses will exceed your income; in consequence you will experience difficulties. Nevertheless, you have the capacity to earn money, particularly when you are able to do the work or to give your attention to those things that vitally interest you. In those directions where you experience enthusiasm, there will be opportunities to bring about developments that can react very favourably upon money matters. On the other hand, there will be occasions when the inclination to make money quickly or easily will be very pronounced and you will need to be very firm with yourself, resisting tendencies towards speculation or the taking of risks in the hope that you will make big money or at least sufficient to enable you to break away from conditions of work or service that do not appeal to you. Do not let yourself be misled by those tendencies, for they can bring future dissolution. Consistent effort will be necessary if you are to get the income that you desire.

The number FOURTEEN will cause you to be practical in the handling of money matters despite the natural impulse shown by Aries rising. It is quite possible that in some way your work or certain of your personal interests and activities will be associated with money matters and quite a deal of trust will be placed in your integrity and honesty. The acquisitive instinct will be marked, and from a normal stand point you will endeavour to conserve your financial interests and to build up a reserve. You will usually weigh up the risks you take, especially as regards speculation and investment, but if the end seems to justify the risk then you will go ahead. If you benefit, you will use the money gained to strengthen your financial position, but if you lose, then you will accept the loss in as philosophical a manner as possible and will be guided by the experience gained, in your future transactions.

Benefit can be derived through activities and interests to do with the artistic side of life, such as music, painting, sculpture; and sometimes through entertainment.

The number FIFTEEN denotes that you will derive money and assist normal income as a result of proper planning and a courageous carrying out of plans. Many of your ideas will be practical but you will need to be firm and watchful to see that others in higher positions do not usurp them and put them over as their own, thus denying you the rightful proceeds. The accepting of authoritative and responsible position will aid the financial side of life and, as a result of thrift you will be able to build up quite a substantial reserve. It is a number that is more favourable for investments than for speculation. At times worrying conditions will arise as a result of delay or through your vocational activities being disturbed by national or international difficulties, but your natural forethought will aid you in working through these periods.

The number SIXTEEN although giving you the capacity to work hard in order to obtain money, shows that though you can obtain very good income through your own work and efforts, it will not be easy to conserve or to save money because there will always be an urge to spend, and at times an inclination to take risks which you will not be able to control. As a result, money will be lost and obligations will be entered into that will cause quite a deal of anxiety in the future. In your case much will depend upon whether you are married or not, and upon the manner in which your partner handles money matters. If your partner is practical, then it will be easier for you to restrain your extravagance and to save, but if your partner is similar to yourself then financial difficulties will become accentuated from time to time.

The number SEVENTEEN indicates that money and income can be derived from more than one source or through the utilising of more than one kind of activity. Thus, whilst the main source of your income can come from your normal work, business or profession, you can develop an auxiliary source that will give you extra money.

Ability of a literary or kindred nature can be employed, interests to do with transport or travel can have some sway over money matters, or there can be a giving of tuition or instruction to others. Fluctuations of income and expenditure will occur; sometimes things will be very good, but there will be occasions when obligations will compel attention and in doing so will create a temporary sense of apprehension. Yet you will always have plenty of new ideas on how to draw in money and, though certain of these will not be practical, a lot of them, if knocked into shape, will be productive of benefit. You should, however, always be cautious both in the making and also while signing financial agreements, and should be aware of all clauses and conditions before taking the final decision.

The number EIGHTEEN will intensify your power of imagination in regard to money and in many instances, will influence your decisions in connection with money matters. You will want to attract money to you, and once you acquire it your tenacity in holding on to it will be very strong, In marked contradiction to your temperamental restlessness and changeability.

Interests of domestic and family nature will have some influence over your decisions and actions and it will not always be easy to follow your own inclinations, particularly if you are married, or in partnership or have sons and/or daughters. Nevertheless, their suggestions should always be listened to, as on occasions they will be of value, either in advancing financial interests or in overcoming difficulties. Benefit will come through property, and sometimes through inheritance. On the other hand, family upsets, squabbles, disputes can react adversely on overall financial affairs, or demands by the marriage partner or other members of the family can cause personal embarrassment.

The number NINETEEN shows you to be very ambitious where money is concerned and you will want to do things so as to have a large income, which in turn will enable you to entertain and to take a prominent part in social and public affairs. Fortunately, your power of organisation is good and thus will aid you in handling of people and affairs that are associated with the financial side of your life. There will, however, be times when extravagant inclinations will require restraining and it will not always be easy to exercise this restraint because of a natural desire to have as many of the good things of life as you can. Unless you do restrain these inclinations you will experience periods when expenditure will exceed income, and as a result, temporary strain and worry will occur until such time as your resourcefulness has enabled you to overcome the difficulties. Speculation and investment will attract you because of the latent possibilities of making money, but it will be essential to maintain practicality and not to lose your sense of proportion. Benefit can be derived, but there are dangers of loss.

The number TWENTY is a helpful number so far as money is concerned, for it draws out personal initiative and enables you to apply personal ability to the acquiring of money. Irrespective of whether your work is mental or manual you will find it relatively easy to adapt your activities to those things from which quite a degree of benefit will be obtained. You will benefit through home and family affairs, as this is a number that is often associated with benefit through inheritance or legacy. The constructive planning of affairs and the maintaining of a practical line of action will always bring you benefit and enable you to create a reserve for future eventualities.

The number TWENTY-ONE is another of the more fortunate numbers and signifies that financial benefits will be derived both through your own initiative and enterprise and as a result of the influence and support of people in influential and authoritative positions, who will be well disposed towards you. In many respects you will have a flair for speculation and investment, although in the former direction a degree of forethought should be exercised and you should not act too much on the spur of the moment. Sometimes matters to do with children and young persons will react very favourably upon overall financial affairs.

The number TWENTY-TWO is a somewhat contrary number in its influence over money. It shows that there will be seasonal fluctuations which can react on your work or your business. On the whole, you have a good sense of the value of money, and though you will not mind spending money, when you have to, you will invariably try to keep a reserve for a rainy day. Conditions of health, both personal and of others in your family, will react upon money interests, and when ill health occurs there will be a loss of income should you be ill yourself, or an incurring of extra-expense if someone else is ill.

Hora System

After studying your lucky number and the Money Number, it would be wise to study the Hora System. "HORA" means the ruling of a particular planet at a particular moment in relation to future results. By employing this Hora System, you will know the auspicious time for a certain act. In fact, it has been observed that clients who visit you in a particular hora have difficulties similar to one another and pertaining to the influencing planet in that hora.

In order to find out the hora at a particular moment, the planets have been arranged in a special chronological order. Each day of the week is named after the planet which rules that day. Thus, Sun rules over Sunday, Moon rules over Monday, Mars rules over Tuesday, Mercury rules over Wednesday, Jupiter rules over Thursday, Venus rules over Friday and Saturn rules over Saturday. This means that the Sun will rule the first hour after sunrise on Sunday, the Moon will rule the first hour after sunrise on Monday and so on.

The circle of 24 hours is divided into day and night. The day of 12 hours is divided into 12 equal parts called planetary hours which are each of equal length of 60 minutes. The planetary enumeration of the hours being at local sunrise, the first hour being ruled by the planet which gives its name to the day, as explained above. This can be tabulated as shown on page 175. Even days of the week are given at the top. Below each day, the hora of the planet is given starting from the first hour after sunrise. The planets ruling the hora are arranged in the following chronological order—Sun, Venus, Mercury, Moon, Saturn, Jupiter and Mars. After Mars, again the hora of Sun starts.

Auspicious Hora According To The Ruling Number

Every number is governed by a particular Rasi (Zodiac) and has auspicious, semi-auspicious or inauspicious hora. This is shown in the table on page 176.

From the above various methods of finding out the auspicious hora we have to combine the hora shown by our ruling number and hora of the hour of the day. This will lead us to achieve success in our efforts in a particular direction.

YOUR LUCKY NUMBER AND MONEY NUMBER

Hour	*Sunday*	*Monday*	*Tuesday*	*Wednesday*	*Thursday*	*Friday*	*Saturday*
1	Sun	Moon	Mars	Mercury	Jupiter	Venus	Saturn
2	Venus	Saturn	Sun	Moon	Mars	Mercury	Jupiter
3	Mercury	Jupiter	Venus	Saturn	Sun	Moon	Mars
4	Moon	Mars	Mercury	Jupiter	Venus	Saturn	Sun
5	Saturn	Sun	Moon	Mars	Mercury	Jupiter	Venus
6	Jupiter	Venus	Saturn	Sun	Moon	Mars	Mercury
7	Mars	Mercury	Jupiter	Venus	Saturn	Sun	Moon
8	Sun	Moon	Mars	Mercury	Jupiter	Venus	Saturn
9	Venus	Saturn	Sun	Moon	Mars	Mercury	Jupiter
10	Mercury	Jupiter	Venus	Saturn	Sun	Moon	Mars
11	Moon	Mars	Mercury	Jupiter	Venus	Saturn	Sun
12	Saturn	Sun	Moon	Mars	Mercury	Jupiter	Venus

The symbols allotted to different planets are as under:

(1) Sun ☉ (2) Venus ♀ (3) Mercury ☿ (4) Moon ☽ (5) Saturn ♄ (6) Jupiter ♃ (7) Mars ♂

Ruling Number	*Rasi*	*Auspicious Hora*	*Semi-auspicious Hora*	*Inauspicious Hora*
9	Aries	Sun, Moon, Mars Jupiter	Venus, Saturn	Mercury
6	Taurus	Mercury, Venus, Saturn	Jupiter, Mars	Sun, Moon
5	Gemini	Sun, Mercury, Venus	Mars, Jupiter, Saturn	Moon
2	Cancer	Sun, Mercury, Moon	Mars, Jupiter, Venus, Saturn	
1	Leo	Sun, Moon, Mars, Jupiter	Mercury	Venus, Saturn
5	Virgo	Sun, Mercury, Venus	Mars, Saturn, Jupiter	Moon
6	Libra	Mercury, Venus, Saturn	Mars, Jupiter	Sun, Moon
9	Scorpio	Sun, Moon, Mars, Jupiter	Venus, Saturn	Mercury
3	Sagittarius	Sun, Moon, Mars, Jupiter	Saturn	Mercury, Venus
8	Capricorn	Mercury, Venus, Saturn	Jupiter	Sun, Moon, Mars
8	Aquarius	Mercury, Venus, Saturn	Jupiter	Sun, Moon, Mars
3	Pisces	Sun, Moon, Mars	Saturn	Mercury, Venus

CHAPTER 16

WHAT'S IN A NAME?

Uptil now we have studied how individual numbers in a given birth date radiate vibrations and how these vibrations heighten one's personality or help one to improve one's lot in life by repeating the lucky numbers indicated by the date of the month. Now I shall explain how name emits certain vibrations and how we can change the vibrations of our name by making a slight change. It is necessary that our birth date, vibrations and those of the name should be in harmony in order to have a smooth sailing in life. People have often come to me complaining that there is always a delay in their life or they do not get the desired or expected results. After studying their cases, I have found that many a time the vibrations thrown out from their birth date and those emitted by their names are not in harmony and therefore the total vibrations of their personality are not powerful. In that case, I have to make a suitable change in the name so that its radiations are in unison with those of the birth-date. It is my experience that the desired results are acquired by making a slight change in the name.

Once a friend of mine, who runs an electronic concern, complained that a big company had promised to purchase all the products of his concern, but somehow even after three years the actual contract could not be finalised. After my suggestion that he add one more letter to his name and to repeat that name several thousand times, He took a paper and a pencil and went on writing his altered name for five to ten minutes everyday. After about three weeks he informed me that he got the result of his repeated vibrations and the agreement was finally signed.

Every name includes a vibratory number so important that it affects the mind and personality of the individual who carries it as well as impresses others. The name of adoption carries with it the number of development which is a new channel that may be developed through life, giving opportunity for individual activity that indicates success or failure. Each single name contains distinct vibrations of its own, such as—

1. This family name, which is the surname, carries the hereditary qualities.
2. The first name is known as the active name which dominates the career of the person.
3. Passive name is the father's or husband's name. When only the initial alphabets of the first name and the father's name are written, they become the passive name, such as V. P. Singh. Here V. P. are passive and 'Singh' becomes active.
4. The destiny name is the full name given at birth.

According to the Hindu System, the first letter of the name has a relation with the Rasi (Zodiac) or Nakshatra (Constellation). Similarly at the time of the marriage, the new name of the wife is determined according to the first letter of the husband's name, so that there would remain harmony between the husband and wife.

It is a practice in some religions that the name of the person, who is on the death bed, is changed so that the evil spirits may not harm the dying person and that he should survive.

In order to find out the name vibrations, each alphabet is allotted a particular number. There are different systems of allotting these numbers to each alphabet. According to the first system, which we are going to adopt, the alphabets and the respective numbers are as under:

Each letter is given a number and it is as follows:

A-1	B-2	C-3	D-4	E-5	F-8
G-3	H-5	I-1	J-1	K-2	L-3
M-4	N-5	O-7	P-8	Q-1	R-2
S-3	T-4	U-6	V-6	W-6	X-5
Y-1	Z-7				

The prefixes, Mr., Mrs., Shri., Smt., etc. are not to be taken into consideration.

In short, each number includes alphabets, as under:

1	:	A,	I,	J,	Q,	Y
2	:	B,	K,	R		
3	:	C,	G,	L,	S	
4	:	D,	M,	T		
5	:	E,	H,	N,	X	
6	:	U,	V,	W		
7	:	O,	Z			
8	:	F,	P.			

According to the second method (which we are not going to adopt) the numbers allotted to each alphabet are as under:

1,	2,	3,	4,	5,	6,	7,	8,	9
A,	B,	C,	D,	E,	F,	G,	H,	I,
J,	K,	L,	M,	N,	O,	P,	Q,	R,
S,	T,	U,	V,	W,	X,	Y,	Z	

In this second method number 9 is taken into consideration whereas in the first system above there is no letter allotted to number 9. We shall now proceed further according to our first system and study the values of the name.

Let us suppose that the name of an individual is RAMESH VISHNU TIWARI. The numerical vibrations of this name are as under:

	RAMESH	VISHNU	TIWARI
	R A M E S H	V I S H N U	T I W A R I
	2 1 4 5 3 5	6 1 3 5 5 6	4 1 6 1 2 1
Total	20	26	15
Single digit	2 +	8 +	6 = 16
			= 7

If the individual always writes his complete name as above, his final vibrations, when reduced to a single digit, are of number 7. If this number 7 is a friend of the number indicated by the date of the month in his birth date, (as shown earlier while dealing with the number seven) he can continue signing his full name. He can also use his full name, on his letter-heads and on his name plate. On the whole, he will sail smoothly through life and his objects will be achieved. This full name is known as the destiny name.

Supposing the full name does not harmonise with the person's birth date, we have then to see whether any other formation of the same is suitable to make the necessary harmony. For instance, let us try the following names:

1. Ramesh V. Tiwari:
   Here the first name is the active name.
2. R. V. Tiwari:
   The first two short forms become passive.

3. R. Tiwari; or
4. Ramesh Tiwari:

   Here both the active name and the family name are powerful.

We should work out numerical values for each of the above combinations and see which is most suitable for the birth-date. In case none of these is suitable or matches the birth-date, we can add one or two letters to the name and alter the spelling. For example, in the first name we can add one more 'm' and write 'Rammesh' or one more 'a' and write 'Ramesha'. If this is also not suitable, we should try the spelling of the word 'Tiwari' as 'Tiwaari'. Instead of letter 'i' at the end we can also spell as 'y'. But the numerical values of 'i' and 'y' are the same, that is one. Therefore using 'y' instead of 'i' would not make any difference. This is how we have to try various combinations in the name and create new vibrations which would finally harmonise with the birth date vibrations and improve the personality of the individual. Once we set right the name vibrations, it is necessary to repeat those vibrations several thousand times every day by writing the name on a paper for some five to ten minutes. I assure my readers that such changes do help the individual to make his life healthy and smooth. I have tried this method hundreds of times in my study.

Mental Vibrations And Material Vibrations

I shall go slightly deeper into our theory of vibrations. In the name vibrations, we can have two parts, one 'mental vibrations' and the other 'material vibrations'. The number values of all the vowels in a name are written at the top and the number values of the remaining letters (consonants) are written at the bottom. By doing so we shall know the mental as well as the material picture of the thoughts of an individual.

For clarification, we shall take the same name which we discussed above, Ramesh Vishnu Tiwari. In this name we have to separate the vowels and the consonants. In the name Ramesh we have two vowels, 'a' and 'e'. So we write the numerical values of these letters at the top and those of the consonants at the bottom. Thus for Ramesh:

$$\frac{1 + 5}{2 + 4 + 3 + 5} = \frac{6}{14}$$

In the name Ramesh the 'mental' vibrations are 6 and of Venus. The 'material' vibrations are 14 i.e. 5 which means Mercury. In short, on the mental plane, Ramesh is governed by Venus. He loves beauty, nature, art, decency and such things as are the characteristics of the planet Venus and number 6.

On the 'material' plane the name Ramesh represents the number 5 and the planet Mercury. He is shrewd, clever and has a business aptitude. He lovers science, research and intellectual work. We can similarly work out the 'mental' and 'material' vibrations from the complete name and find out the total personality.

If a man wishes to start a business we can suggest a suitable name for his enterprise. An auspicious name can be suggested for a house or for a building. An appropriate name can be given to a newly born baby, and so on. It is said that Napoleone Buonapart made a slight change in his name and he became the Emperor.

We may add up the total vibrations in a name (Destiny Name) and bring it to a single digit. In the name 'Ramesh Vishnu Tiwari' taken above the total vibrations work out to 61. When this total is reduced to a single digit, it comes to 7. The meaning of different numbers arrived at by this method is as under:

1. It rules the brain and the mind and gives good intellectual capacity. It is associated with learning, education and the teaching or training of others. There is a capacity for writing and certain forms of literary work, for journalism and contact with news papers.

2. It gives you a natural power of discrimination and perception which will express itself in a natural manner through business and associated channels. You can carry out any routine set out by others and when necessary, can evolve a routine of your own proving satisfactory to all concerned.

3. This number gives you a strong desire for peace and harmony, and the sensitivity to any thing of a deliberately discordant nature. You are naturally courteous and desirous of being on good terms with other people.

4. This number gives you a degree of result and in certain respects will cause you to be secretive, although this will not necessarily interfere with your everyday associations. You will express more resistance and fighting capacity than those around you may recognise, and should anyone attempt to take unfair advantage of you they will be extremely surprised at the resistance you will put up for the protection of your own interests.

5. It gives you a broad and tolerant view upon life and will strengthen your spirit of comradeship. Religious and philosophical matters will appeal to you, there will be a strong desire for travel and it is possible for the missionary spirit to be strong.

6. This number is ruled by the planet of affection, of love and of beauty. This will cause your desire for companionship to be exceedingly strong and, therefore, all matters to do with the affections, with marriage and with

friendships will prove to be very important and a great deal of your happiness or unhappiness in life will depend upon the nature of the ties and associations which you form,

7. This makes you frank and outspoken with a very strong desire for liberty and freedom of thought and action, as well as for maintaining personal independence.

8. It makes you ambitious practical and in some ways acquisitive. You will also experience difficulties when you want others to carry out work for you. Sometimes you will know what it is to feel depressed and unhappy and will temporarily lose heart and wonder if there is any thing in life worth living for.

9. It shows that you are thoughtful, reflective and studious. Many of your thoughts and ideas will be in advance of those of your companions and yet will not interfere with your friendships and associations. In fact you will find that those with whom you associate will often look to you for advice regarding their problems.

Predictive aspect from name

One of the most interesting forms of the kabalism of numbers is that which relates names to incidents by means of the numerical value of letters.

To each letter of the alphabet a unit value is given, the valuation following the Hebrew code, as already given. These values are then multiplied by the inverse order of the letters, the products being finally added together. The unit value of the sum of these products constitutes the "kabalistic key number". This key number being referred to the Tarot, an interpretation is obtained.

Each of the Tarotic numbers has a fourfold interpretation,

namely a spiritual, intellectual, psychic, and physical, the correspondence running through from the world of principles to that of causes, thence to the world of effects, terminating in the world of ultimates, which is the concrete world of Physical Phenomena.

The full interpretation of the twenty two Major keys of the Tarot is given on page 22. The method followed by this Kabalism will easily be understood by the following example:

R	A	J	I	V		G	A	N	D	H	I
2	1	1	1	6		3	1	5	4	5	1

The name 'Rajiv' contains 5 letters. Put this number at the top and then go on writing one below another the inverse number starting from 5 thus:

5
4
3
2
1

Then multiply each of the above numbers by the number allotted to each of the alphabet in the name 'Rajiv' starting from R. It will work out as under:

5 × 2-R	=	10
4 × 1-A	=	4
3 × 1-J	=	3
2 × 1-I	=	2
1 × 6-V	=	6
		25 = 7

The name Gandhi has 6 letters. If we work out this name on the above basis, the result is as under:

6 × 3-G	=	18	
5 × 1-A	=	5	
4 × 5-N	=	20	
3 × 4-D	=	12	
2 × 5-H	=	10	
1 × 1-I	=	1	
		66	= 12

The interpretation of the whole name Rajiv Gandhi is as follows (see page 18)—

1. Rajiv = 7 = *The Chariot*
   Help, providence, also war, triumph, presumption, vengeance, trouble.

2. Gandhi = 12 = *The Hanged Man*
   Wisdom, circumspection, discernment, trials, sacrifice, intuition, prophecy.

3. For the full name, we have 7 + 12 = 19
   19 = *The Sun*
   Material happiness, fortunate marriage, contentment.

Now you can interpret the final significance of the name Rajiv Gandhi as under:

The name shows that he will have to undergo troubles due to certain things presumed by him. This presumption may lead him to fight against vengeance, involving war-like measures. His good intentions will receive help from foreign countries and will help him to overcome the opposition. (All this interpretation is based on the name Rajiv, signifying number 7.)

He will have to exert his will power and employ his wisdom, discernment and prophetic vision. He will have to sacrifice some of his deep rooted interests.

Finally when we add together both the names, we come to number 19. It means that at the end of his mission, Rajiv Gandhi will obtain success and happiness after going through several ordeals.

I will now explain the significance of this name according to Pythagorean theory. Please refer to page 19.

1. The vibrations of Rajiv are 7
2. The vibrations of Gandhi are 12

We have to arrange this number as 712.

We have now to look to the interpretation of number 700 and then refer to number 12.

The meaning is as under:

700 Might, dominion, authority

12 A fortunate writing, a town or city.

We can interpret that Rajiv Gandhi will acquire great authority and will dominate the Congress Party. He will develop contacts with other powers through agreements and contracts.

We can also work out the significance of the name Rajiv Gandhi according to the meaning attached to compound numbers and as described in Chapter 18.

R	2	G	3
A	1	A	1
J	1	N	5
I	1	D	4
V	6	H	5
		I	1
	11		19

11 + 19 = 30.

You have now to read the interpretation given to number 30, which is as follows: (see page 203)

"This is a number of thoughtful deduction, retrospection and mental superiority over one's fellow, but as it seems to belong completely to the mental plane, the persons it represents are likely to put all material things on one side—not because they have to, but because they wish to do so. For this reason it is neither fortunate nor unfortunate, for either depends on the mental outlook of the person it represents. It can be all powerful, but it is just as often indifferent according to the will or desire of the person."

CHAPTER 17

SIGNIFICANCE OF ALPHABETS A TO Z

Each letter of the alphabet is the symbol of a concept and has its own numerical value. Every word therefore conveys a story when you know the meaning of each alphabet. Your name reveals your born and hidden characteristics, your likes and dislikes.

In order to understand a name in all its details, we will now study the meaning of each alphabet.

1. **A:** It denotes creative talent, initiative and leadership. If it is the first alphabet in your name, it shows a strong will power and determination. If A is the first vowel in your name, following a consonant, it shows a dominating nature. The speciality of the capital letter A is the cross bar joining the two slanting lines of the letter. It is a sign of ambition. It indicates a desire to climb up the ladder of life.

2. **B:** This letter is enclosed and completes a circuit. It signifies that you keep your inner thoughts to yourself and only few friends will share your confidence. You are moody and emotional. It takes some time for you to mix with strangers. When your name starts with B, you are cooperative and like to follow the suggestions given by others. If B is the first consonant in your name after following a vowel, you are introspective and understand yourself as well as others.

3. **C:** If this is the first letter of your name, you have intellectual abilities. You have a healthy outlook on life. If this

comes as the first consonant after a vowel, it gives you optimistic ideas. If this letter is repeated often, it means you will finally obtain success and overcome difficulties. You are very active and energetic. You are happy only when you are occupied. You also have a negative side to your personality. When your mind is filled with fear or anxiety, you should try to develop resistance to the worrying habit.

4. **D:** This letter is similar to that of B, in the sense that this letter is also enclosed and completed by a circuit. You are therefore self sufficient and keep your inner thoughts to yourself. You attach great importance to material things. The meaning of this enclosed letter is that you should rise above your enclosure and forget that you are bound by material barriers. If this alphabet occurs more than twice in your name, it symbolises limitations on your activities which, however, you will overcome by your tolerance and patience.

5. **E:** If your name starts with this letter, you have a marked ability to write and speak. You activate every thing you come in contact with. This alphabet is mental and intellectual and produces energy and excitement. If this letter is repeated in your name, you acquire fame through writing or oratory. This letter has 3 cross lines representing activity on the spiritual, mental and material level. It shows a balanced character. You look more to the future than to the past. You are interested in making your personal contacts manifold and varied.

6. **F:** If your name starts with this letter, you show love for children and domestic life. You are stubborn and will never tolerate disloyalty. You are fond of quiet and simple pleasures of home life. You like to share the responsibilities of home life. If this letter is repeated in your name, it gives you protection in all family matters.

7. **G:** This letter curves inside upon itself. You love self analysis, meditation and introspection. If this letter is repeated, you are a clever analyst. You understand the motives of others and can go to the bottom of their intentions. You have a sort of intuition and can develop psychic powers. You are thorough in whatever you do. Ideas often take shape in the mind without any previous chain of reasoning. These ideas are generally sound and attention to them will help obviate delays and difficulties. It is necessary to check your impulsive nature and hurry, otherwise you may not get the best result.

8. **H:** This letter has two perpendicular lines with a cross bar in the centre joining the two lines. This figure, therefore, stands firm and well balanced. If your name starts with this letter, you have a level-headed attitude to life, and others can rely upon you. This shows you are kind but you give the impression that you are hard and resolute.

The two perpendicular lines show two directions, up and down. You have the choice within you of either rising or descending the scale of life. You have strong potentialities for material progress at the same time there are strong possibilities of making errors on the material plane.

9. **I:** If your name starts with this letter, it shows your interest for the welfare of others. It shows psychic powers, universal tolerance and sympathy. If this letter is repeated in your name, it signifies extreme sensitivity, and hence suffering. You have communication with far-away places. This letter indicates an alert and alive disposition. You are impatient over delays. You are self reliant and have a tendency to lay down the law. Beliefs and feelings are of an usually intense character. You have an ability to carry on against opposition.

10. **J:** If your name starts with this letter or is the first consonant in the name, you like to find out new associations. You take pride in being in touch with the very latest developments. You are quick to seize new ideas. Usually, you have a bright outlook and you have talent for writing or painting. You divert your attention from one subject to another and herein lies your weakness not to pursue a subject for a long time.

This is the 10th letter and therefore you have many of the qualities shown by number 1. On the whole, you have leadership, prosperity and success in life. You have a magnetic personality and you follow intellectual pursuits and cultural activities.

11. **K:** If this is the first alphabet in your name, you have vivid and magnetic personality. You are cooperative and have endurance. You like all forms of entertainments, theatres and public enterprises. This letter is written in up and down motion and signifies moodiness.

12. **L:** This letter is formed by two lines, a perpendicular one and the other horizontal. The perpendicular line shows aspirations and the horizontal one means the material world. You, therefore, have an ability to reason along clear and distinct lines and also have developed good logic. You are eager to assimilate facts, but are more reserved in accepting theories associated with them. If this is first letter in your name, you have versatility, social popularity and success. Your intuitive faculty assists you in time of need. It gives you a keen insight into the motives of other people. You have an active life with much movement.

13. **M:** When your name starts with this letter, you have strength of character, ability to study and an orderly mind. This letter is the mason of the alphabets and builds story

upon story in its efforts and have noble ideals. If this letter is repeated in your name, you will never accept defeat. You are moody but at the same time you have the other matter-of-fact side.

14. **N:** If this is the first letter in your name, you are intellectual but inconsistent. You will discard as much as you take in, if you cannot progress or advance by your intake. You will be endowed with fluidity but you have a tendency to scatter many of your talents. You do things by fits and starts and have a strong emotional nature. Luck comes in cycles. There are times when nothing appears to go right; at other times, almost anything you take up is successful.

15. **O:** This is a completely enclosed letter and symbolises that you are capable of keeping your inner thoughts very much to yourself. You give greater emphasis on beauty, form and order. You have a tendency to suffer from frequent depressions. Your attitude is conservative and in adverse circumstances you will always exaggerate the difficulties or delays. If this is the first letter in your name, it endows you with intellectuality, balance and the ability to handle your problems. Home, children and affection are the main points of interest in your life.

16. **P:** This letter indicates clarity of mental vision and foresight. You take great delight in preserving and protecting your ego and its development. If there are many P's in your name, power and success follow you. This power may be for good or bad and it is necessary to control the evil and it can be sought through meditation and concentration. The letter P is also another letter which is enclosed and others will never know about your hidden feelings. You will pass off an embarrassing or unpleasant situation without disclosing just how deeply it has affected you. You like to stand away from

the crowd and realise that there is much to be gained by preserving your own individual taste unaffected by others' influences. Whatever your career in life, you succeed in retaining this characteristic of separateness.

17. **Q:** If this is the first letter in your name, it gives you strong will-power and determination. Your routine is set and seldom will you give a despair. You never lose hope even though there is a slight possibility of gaining your objective. You are more successful in organising the affairs of other people than your own. Your mind is always on the lookout for new vistas.

18. **R:** If this letter appears as the first letter in your name, it shows great strength of will which can be used for good or bad. It is necessary for you to use your discretion before exercising your power. You will give advice very freely though you are slow to accept one. You have to understand and make allowance for the difficulties of others which will help you to unburden their worries.

19. **S:** If this is the first letter in your name, it gives you the capacity to make firm friendships and enter into others' lives and interests. You will choose only a particular folk, but if you find that you are betrayed, you will be greatly hurt. Though you have the feeling that some adjustment is necessary, but find it difficult to find out the way to it.

20. **T:** If this is the first letter in your name, it symbolises sacrifice. You do acts of great self denial. You like to hold yourself back in order that the others' interests which may be conflicting with yours, do not embarrass him. You are, therefore, ready to share your success and also distribute your favours very freely. The letter "T" with its perpendicular line and bar at the top, shows aspirations of a spiritual character. You are anxious not only to satisfy your own higher ambitions,

but also to bring happiness into the lives of others. Due to this broad outlook you often meet with frustration. This letter is the twentieth letter from 'A' and its single digit is 2 which represents Moon. It therefore signifies cooperation shown by number 2 and intensified ten times by being followed by the zero. It denotes a nature whose stress is towards the feminine principle of building up the foundation laid by another—of following rather than leading. The letter "T" represents devotion; it is more blessed to give than to receive.

21. **U:** This letter is open at the top wherein the gifts of imagination, charm, inspiration and romance are poured. It means that you will receive many gifts in life but you have to take care that those gifts are retained and preserved properly, otherwise they will flow over as the letter is open at the top. You suffer from anticipating troubles that never materialise.

22. **V:** If this is the first letter in your name, your main characteristic is that you are highly respective. You find little difficulty in grasping and learning anything you set your mind upon. This letter is related to those who often occupy positions of high command and use their powers with discretion. It denotes hard work but also gratifying rewards. You have the ability to bring your master plan or your theory into practice.

23. **W:** If this is the first letter in your name, you experience change in life from old conditions to new ones. You have wavering emotions. It is indicative of the necessity to learn to be dynamic. You have a love of speed, travel, words, excitement, adventures and all that is dramatic and swiftly moving. There will be no limits to your ambitions. Whatever you attempt, you will want to do thoroughly. You will be led to take great risks, having an eager, questioning spirit that wants to taste life in all its phases. The letter "W"

symbolises vanity. But in a well developed character, it is indicative of unusual power.

24. **X:** If this is the first letter in your name you suffer from frequent fits of depression. In adverse circumstances, you will exaggerate your difficulties and delays. You have an attractive personality and your general outlook is conservative. The letter "X" denotes the law of responsibility on the highest or spiritual plane.

25. **Y:** The symbol of the letter "Y" is the diviner, the rod with forked tip, which is used for the discovery of oil or water under the surface of the earth. This letter gives you a desire for the search of esoteric or mystic elements of life. This letter endows you with the desire to search for secrets into the doctrine "behind the veil". You like to keep your thoughts and emotions to yourself and you dislike crowds. You crave independence and freedom. Whatever your situation in life, you always retain this characteristic of separateness.

26. **Z:** If this is the first letter in your name you have a very resolute character. You have a tendency to form fixed habits. Once your mind has decided a particular course, it will not be shaken. You have a great capacity to maintain steady effort, even in the face of several obstructions. Your advice and assistance are frequently sought and wisely respected. You have tremendous potentialities which can be used for either good or bad.

We have discussed above the interplay of influences derived from the first alphabet in your name. It would be quite interesting to analyse each letter in your name and find out the result.

CHAPTER 18

SIGNIFICANCE OF COMPUND NUMBERS

In earlier chapters we have discussed single numbers from one to nine. Now we shall proceed to consider the occult symbolism given to "double" or "compound" numbers and how such knowledge may be used in everyday life.

Though this is a much more advanced and more difficult part of the study of numbers, I will try to explain it in as simple a language as possible.

You are aware that the single numbers denote what you appear to be in the eyes of others, while the double or compound numbers show the hidden influences that play a role behind the schemes and in some mysterious way often foreshadow the future,

When we pass the root numbers from 1 to 9, what is called the greater symbolism of numbers commences and continues until 5 times 9 is reached, or the symbol 45. At this point the mystical number of 7 is brought into operation and added to the number 45, producing 52, which stands for the 52 weeks of a year. This number of 52, multiplied by 7, gives 364 as the ordinary days of the year. The ancients who developed this calculation, used the 365th day of each year as one great festival holiday of all, and no work of any kind was allowed to be done by anybody. This number of 365 is based on the passage of the sun through the twelve divisions of the Zodiac. All the numbers from 10 upwards, become compound numbers and have a meaning of their own distinct from the root number. We do not know how and in what age these compound numbers were discovered. We can only say that they appear to have always existed. The meanings ascribed to the numbers 1 to 9 belongs to the physical or material side of things and compound numbers from 10 onwards belong to the more occult or spiritual side of life. Distinct symbolism has been given to the compound numbers up to that mysterious number of 52.

The universally accepted symbolism of the compound numbers in ancient times was given in pictures and may still be found in the Tarot Cards which have been handed down to us from ancient times and whose origin is lost in antiquity. (Please refer to page 22).

10 Symbolised as the "Wheel of Fortune". It is a number of honour, of faith and self confidence, of rise and fall, one's name will be known for good or evil, according to one's desires; it is a fortunate number in the sense that one's plans are likely to be carried out.

11 This is an ominous number to occultists. It gives warning of hidden dangers, trial and treachery from others. It has a symbol of a "Clenched Hand", and "a Lion Muzzled", and of a person who will have great difficulties to contend against.

12 The symbolism of this number is suffering and anxiety of mind. It is also indicated as "the Sacrifice" or "the Victim" and generally foreshadows one being sacrificed for the plans or intrigues of others.

13 This is a number indicating change of plans, place and as such is not unfortunate, as is generally supposed. In some of the ancient writings it is said, "He who understands the numbers 13 will be given power and dominion". It is

symbolised by the ;picture of a "Skeleton" of "Death", with a scythe reaping down men, in a field of new grown grass where young faces and heads appear cropping up on every side. It is a number of upheaval and destruction. It is a symbol of "Power" which if wrongly used will wreak destruction upon oneself. It is a number of warning of the unknown or unexpected, if it becomes a "compound" number in one's calculations.

14 This is a number of movement, combination of people and things, and danger from natural forces such as tempests, water, air or fire. This number is fortunate for dealings with money, speculation and changes in business, but there is always a strong element of risk and danger attached to it, but generally owing to the actions and foolhardiness of others. If this number comes out in calculations of future events the person should be warned to act with caution and prudence.

15 This is a number of occult significance, of magic and mystery; but as a rule it does not represent the higher side of occultism, its meaning being that the persons represented by it will use every art of magic they can to carry out their purpose. If associated with a good or fortunate single number, it can be very lucky and powerful, but if associated with one of the peculiar numbers, such as a 4 or an 8, the person it represents will not hesitate to use any sort of art, or even "black magic", to gain what he or she desires.

It is peculiarly associated with "good talkers", often with eloquence, gifts of music and art and a dramatic personality, combined with a certain voluptuous temperament and strong personal magnetism. For obtaining money, gifts, and favours from others it is a fortunate number.

16 This number has a most peculiar occult symbolism. It is pictured by "a Tower Struck by Lightening from which a man is falling with a Crown on his head". It is also called "the Sheltered Citadel".

It gives warning of some strange fatality awaiting one, also danger of accidents and defeat of one's plans. If it appears as a "compound" number relating to the future, it is a warning sign that should be carefully noted and plans made in advance in the endeavour to avert its fatalistic tendency.

17 This is a highly spiritual number, and is expressed in symbolism by the 8-pointed Star of Venus; a symbol of "Peace and love". It is also called "the Star of the Magi" and expresses that the person it represents has risen superior in spirit to the trials and difficulties of his life or his career. It is considered a "Number of immortality" and that the person's name "lives after him". It is a fortunate number if it works out in relation to future events, provided it is not associate with the single number of fours and eights.

18 This number has a difficult symbolism to translate. It is pictured as "a rayed moon from which drops of blood are falling; a wolf and a hungry dog are seen below catching the falling drops of blood in their opened mouths, while still lower a crab is seen hastening to join them". It is symbolic of materialism striving to destroy the spiritual side of the nature. It generally associates a person with bitter quarrels, even family ones, also with war, social upheavals, revolutions, and in some cases it indicates making money and position through wars or by wars. It is however a warning of treachery, deception by others, also danger from the elements such as storms, danger from water, fires and explosions. When this "compound" number appears in working out dates in advance, such a date should be taken with a great amount of care, caution and circumspection.

19 This number is regarded as fortunate and extremely favourable. It is symbolised as "the Sun" and is called "the Prince of Heaven". It is a number promising happiness, success, esteem and honour and promises success in one's plan for the future.

20 This number is called "the Awakening"; also "the Judgement". It is symbolised by the figure of a winged angel sounding a trumpet, while from below a man, a women, and a child are seen rising from a tomb with their hands clasped in prayer.

This number has a peculiar interpretation; the call to action, but for some great purpose, cause or duty. It is not a material number and consequently is a doubtful one as far as worldly success is concerned.

If used in relation to a future event, it denotes delays, hindrances to one's plans, which can only be conquered through the development of the spiritual side of nature.

21 This number is symbolised by the picture of "the Universe", and it is also called "the Crown of the Magi". It is a number of advancement, honours, elevation in life and general success. It means victory after long initiation and tests of determination. It is a fortunate number of promise if it appears in any connection with future events.

22 This number is symbolised by a "a Good Man blinded by the folly of others, with a knapsack on his back full of Arrows". In this picture he appears to offer no defence against a ferocious tiger which is attacking him. It is a warning number of illusion and delusion, a good person who lives in a fool's paradise; a dreamer of dreams who awakens only when surrounded by danger. It is also a number of false judgement owing to the influence of others.

As a number in connection with future events, it is a warning and its meaning would be carefully noted.

23 This number is called "the Royal Star of the Lion". It is a promise of success, help from superiors and protection from those in high places. In dealing with future events it is a most fortunate number and a promise of success of one's plans.

24 This number is also fortunate; it promises the assistance and association of those of rank and position with one's plans; it also denotes gain through love and the opposite sex; it is a favourable number when it comes out in relation to future events.

25 This is a number denoting strength gained through experience, and benefits obtained through observation of people and things. It is not deemed exactly "lucky", as its success is given through strife and trials in an earlier life. It is favourable when it appears in regard to the future.

26 This number is full of the gravest warnings for the future. It foreshadows disasters brought about by association with others; ruin by bad speculations, by partnerships, unions and bad advice.

If it comes out in connection with future events one should carefully consider the path one is treading.

27 This is a good number and is symbolised as "the Sceptre". It is a promise of authority, power and command. It indicates that reward will come from the productive intellect; that the creative faculties have shown good seeds that will reap a harvest. Person with this "command" number at their back should carry out their own ideas and plans. It is a fortunate number if it appears in any connection with future events.

28 This number is full of contradictions. It indicates a person of great promise and possibilities who is likely to see all taken away from him unless he carefully provides for the future. It indicates loss through trust in others, opposition and competition in trade, danger of loss through law, and the likelihood of having to begin life's road over and over again.

It is not a fortunate number for the indication of future events.

29 This number indicates uncertainties, treachery, and deception of others; it foreshadows trials, tribulation and unexpected dangers, unreliable friends, and grief and deception caused by members of the opposite sex. It gives grave warning if it comes out in anything concerning future events.

30 This is a number of thoughtful deduction, retrospection, and mental superiority over one's fellows, but as it seems to belong completely to the mental plane, the persons it represents, are likely to put all material things on one side—not because they have to, but because they wish to do so. For this reason it is neither fortunate nor unfortunate, for either depends on the mental outlook of the person it represents. It can be all powerful, but it is just as often indifferent according to the will or desire of the person.

31 This number is very similar to the preceding one, except that the person it represents is even more self contained, lonely, and isolated from his fellows. It is not a fortunate number from a worldly or material stand point.

32 This number has a magical power like the single 5, or the "command" numbers 14 and 23. It is usually associated with combinations of people or nations. It is a fortunate number if the person it represents holds to his own judgement and opinions; if not, his plans are likely to be wrecked by the

stubbornness and stupidity of others. It is a favourable number if it appears in connection with future events.

33 This number has no potency of its own and consequently has the same meaning as 24—which is also a 6—and the next to it in its own series of "compound" numbers.

34 Has the same meaning as the number 25, which is the one next to it in its own series of "compound" numbers.

35 Has the same meaning as the number 26, which is the one next to it in its own series of "compound" numbers.

36 Has the same meaning as the number 27, which is the one next to it in its own series of "compound" numbers.

37 This number has a distinct potency of its own. It is a number of good and fortunate friendships in love, and in combinations connected with the opposite sex. It is also good for partnerships of all kinds. It is a fortunate indication if it appears in connection with future events.

38 Has the same meaning as the number 29, which is the one next to it in its own series of "compound" numbers.

39 Has the same meaning as the number 30, which is the one next to it in its own series of "compound" numbers.

40 Has the same meaning as the number 31, which is the one next to it in its own series of "compound" numbers.

41 Has the same meaning as the number 32, which is the one next to it in its own series of "compound" numbers.

42 Has the same meaning as the number 24.

43 This is an unfortunate number. It is symbolised by the signs of revolution, upheaval, strife, failure, and prevention

and is not a fortunate number if it comes out in calculation relating to future events.

44 Has the same meaning as the number 26.

45 Has the same meaning as the number 27.

46 Has the same meaning as the number 37.

47 Has the same meaning as the number 29.

48 Has the same meaning as the number 30.

49 Has the same meaning as the number 31.

50 Has the same meaning as the number 32..

51 This number has a very powerful potency of its own. It represents the nature of the warrior, it promises sudden advancement in whatever one undertakes, it is especially favourable for those in military or naval life and for leaders in any cause. At the same time it threatens enemies, dangers and the likelihood of assassination.

52 Has the same meaning as 43.

We have now completed the 52 numbers which represent the 52 weeks of our year, and for all practical purposes there is no necessity to proceed further. I will now show the method of employing the symbolism of these "compound" numbers together with the "single" numbers whose meaning you have learned earlier.

The rule to follow is" You must add the date you wish to know about to the total of the compound numbers of your name, see what number this gives you and read its meaning given above.

Example: Let us suppose that you wish to know if, say Monday the 26th April will be a favourable day for you to carry out some plan; let us say, to ask for a rise in your position or in your wages. Take the numbers given to each letter of your name as shown on page 179 add to the total "compound" number or its single digit the number given by the addition of the 26th April, 2 + 6 = 8, add this 8 to the total of your Name number and Birth number and look up the meaning given to the final number produced and you will find at once whether Monday, the 26th will be favourable to you or not. If you see that it does not give a fortunate number, then add the next day, the 27th or the next until you come to a date that is indicated as favourable. Act on the favourable date thus shown and you will find that the day thus indicated will be fortunate for you.

Let us suppose that your name is RAJIV GANDHI and that your birth date is 13th May.

R	- 2	G	- 3
A	- 1	A	- 1
J	- 1	N	- 5
I	- 1	D	- 4
V	- 6	H	- 5
		I	- 1
	11 = 2		19 = 10
			= 1

Example: You now add 2 and 1 which gives you 3. To this 3 you add 8 produced by similar means from the 26th April. This gives you the compound number 11 (3 + 8), which when reduced to the single digit gives you 2. Now add to this the date of your birth 13, which produces 15 as the last compound number.

Now look up the meaning given to the compound number 15 which reads "for obtaining money, gifts and favours from others, it is a favourable number". Therefore the occult influences playing on your name "Rajiv Gandhi", as born on 13th May, would be favourable on the 26th April for your using that date to ask favours or to carry out your plans. If this date does not give you favourable indications, you should then work out the 27th April, or the next day or the next, until you find a date indicated as favourable.

By adopting another approach to the significance of the name and its compound numbers, we can have another meaning for the name Rajiv Gandhi. The total vibrations of the name Rajiv come to 11 and that of the name Gandhi come to 19. That means the total number of the name is 30 and we have to read the meaning attached to this compound number which is as follows:

"This is a number of thoughtful deduction, retrospection and mental superiority over one's fellows but as it seams to belong completely to the mental plane, the persons it represents are likely to put all material things on one side—not because they have to, but because they wish to do so. For this reason it is neither fortunate nor unfortunate, for either depends on the mental outlook of the person it represents. It can be all powerful but it is just as often indifferent according to the will or desire of the persons."

CHAPTER 19

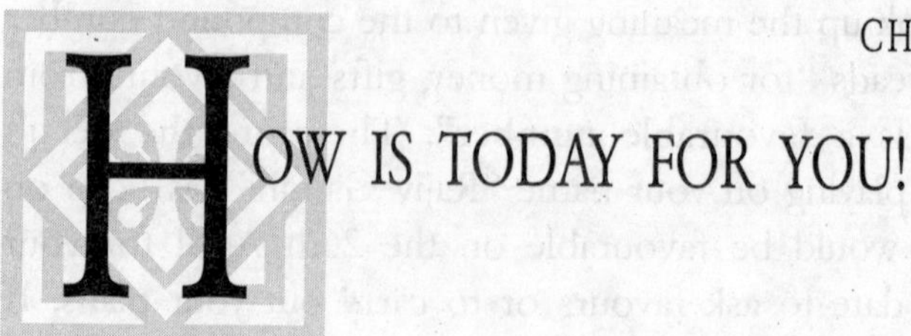

HOW IS TODAY FOR YOU!

As we refer to an almanac for a 'muhurth' or an auspicious day, numerology can help us to know what day is good for a specific act. We are interested in knowing whether a day is good or not for a particular act, for instance, we want to ask for a favour, or we want to enter into a contract, or we want to embark on a journey, or to start a new course of study, etc. We have already discussed one method of finding out the auspicious date from the compound number as explained in the previous chapter. According to the study of numerology, there is another system whereby we can find out a lucky day for a certain step.

We have to take only the date and the month in our birth date and add them to the total of the digits, of the date of a particular day. Supposing the date of birth is 16-1-1965 and today is 13-12-1985. We have to work it out as under:

The first date	16	
Add the month January	1	
Add todays' date	13	
Add present month	12	
Add the year	1985	
Total	2027	= 11 = 2

Number 2 is auspicious for certain acts of ours. Please read the explanation given to Number 2. In this way you have to calculate each day. I shall give below the significance of these numbers from 1 to 9 and we should choose the right day for our step. Supposing we want to take legal advice, number 3 is auspicious for that act. According to the above example, today is the day of number 2. Therefore, for taking legal advice we should select the next day. Every day is favourable to certain kinds of activity and we should take our action on the proper day.

Significance Of Numbers From One To Nine

No. 1: *Vibrations emitted by number 1 are favourable for:*

(1) Planning ambitious projects
(2) Expressing novel ideas
(3) Starting some original work
(4) Enrolling for a language course
(5) Developing a new friendship
(6) Interview with a new boss
(7) Participation in music and artistic activities
(8) Purchasing machinery and equipment
(9) Trying for a competition or election
(10) Going on a journey.

No. 2: *Vibrations emitted by number 2 are favourable for:*

(1) Improving financial status
(2) Selecting a life partner
(3) Trying to get co-operation from others
(4) Entering into a contract
(5) Gaining another's confidence
(6) Diplomatic talk and discrimination.

No. 3: *Vibrations emitted by number 3 are favourable for:*

(1) Furthering your ambition
(2) Going in for presentation articles

(3) Taking legal advice
(4) Making new investments
(5) Trying for a favour or assistance
(6) Presenting credentials
(7) Studying a new subject
(8) Developing contacts with editors.

No. 4: *Vibrations emitted by number 4 are favourable for:*

(1) Providing educational facilities for children
(2) Entering into a contract
(3) Fixing securities
(4) Arranging home affairs
(5) Consulting a doctor
(6) Dealing with agriculture.

No. 5: *Vibrations emitted by number 5 are favourable for:*

(1) Playing with children
(2) Participating in a garden party
(3) Attending to correspondence
(4) Making new acquaintances or friendships
(5) Giving a talk on the radio
(6) Arranging a short trip.

No. 6: *Vibrations emitted by number 6 are favourable for:*

(1) Making yourself attractive and charming
(2) Developing love contacts
(3) Visiting a beauty parlour
(4) Proposing marriage
(5) Patching up old quarrels
(6) Taking rest and reading books
(7) Attending a conference.

No. 7: *Vibrations emitted by number 7 are favourable for:*

(1) Controlling unwanted talk
(2) Taking care about diet
(3) Peace and meditation
(4) Developing psychic studies
(5) Taking decisions about family matters
(6) Adopting a child
(7) Consulting a Guru or a spiritual authority.

No. 8: *Vibrations emitted by number 8 are favourable for:*

(1) Studying mysticism
(2) Acquiring power of intuition
(3) Developing spiritual healing
(4) Making love
(5) Trying one's luck in a race or a lottery
(6) Donations to charitable institutions
(7) Contesting an election
(8) Looking after financial matters

No. 9: *Vibrations emitted by number 9 are favourable for:*

(1) Visiting charitable institutions
(2) Dealing with confidential documents
(3) Practising spiritual healing
(4) Earning fame and reputation
(5) Rectifying old mistakes
(6) Going on a journey or a picnic
(7) Doing original work
(8) Visiting musical concerns.

A few years ago an officer from the army called on me one Sunday and informed me that he was expecting orders from his Head Quarters at Delhi for his transfer to Nagaland. He had been stationed in Poona for six or seven years and naturally had arranged for the education of his two daughters in Poona up to the tenth standard. His immediate transfer would disturb his family life and so he was very uneasy about his transfer. I worked out the next three or four days according to the formula we have studied above. The next day fell under the vibration of number 3. I advised him to contact his Headquarters and request that his transfer be postponed by a few months till the examinations of his daughters were over. I also worked out the day next to that which came under the vibration of number 4 which favours 'arranging home affairs' or 'providing educational facilities for the children'. I therefore predicted that most probably he would get his orders under number 4. He returned to me after about 6 days and told me that he received the orders on the day predicted and that he would be proceeding to Nagaland in a month of two.

In addition to the favourable day, if our lucky number also falls on that day, it will achieve positive results for the action taken on that day.

I request my readers to try this method when taking decisions on different matters and to keep a regular note and see the results for themselves. I am sure that they will achieve success.

CHAPTER 20

HOW IS THIS MONTH FOR YOU!

In the last chapter we studied about the auspicious days for particular actions. We shall now study about the month and work out for what specific purpose that month is auspicious.

In this system we have to take into consideration the date, the month and the year in your birth-date. To this, you have to add the number of the current month (the month in which you are solving this problem) and the number of months after your last birth date. Let us suppose that your birth-date is 14-9-1962. let us suppose that the current month is May 1988. You have to solve this example as under:

Date of your Birth	14
Month of your Birth	9
Year of your Birth	1962
No. of current month	5
No. of months after your last birth-date (i.e. from September 1987 to May 1988)	8
	1998

Reduce this total to a single digit which is 9.

Thus, the month of May 1988 would be a 9 individual month cycle. Please read the explanation given to number 9.

In this way you have to calculate for each month what you want to know about. The significance from number 1 to 9 would be as under:

No. 1 Month

This is a good month for new business enterprises, new associations and new ideas. You should concentrate on buying and selling, advertising, publicity and creative work for profit. Number 1 denotes the opening of a new cycle. Individuality, initiative and independence are prominent in this month. Leadership and forcefulness bring success and achievement. You may expect new friendship which may prove a source of pleasure to you. Social success should bring you happiness and popularity. The new strength arising within you revitalizes your personality.

No. 2 Month

This is the month of co-operation rather than to start any new project. Yours will be the role of the matchmaker and the one to reconcile those who have quarrelled. Keep your temper at an even level. A friendship may blossom into a romance, or may turn into a prosperous collaboration. Minor changes may take place in your routine but these will come as a result of the suggestions of others. In this month you may find that you are unable to make up your mind about a vital issue. In that case please postpone your decision until the next month.

No. 3 Month

Be careful not to squander your money, as a temptation to play may be very strong. As a leader of your group, you may find yourself in great prestige. In this month you may get increased pleasure and appreciation in arts, particularly in literature. You will express yourself through words and oratory. You will experience optimism and prosperity during this month.

No. 4 Month

You have to work hard and then achieve success in this month. This is the month for saving and building up for the future. Bring out the ideas that you have been fostering and express them now or prepare a campaign that will bear fruit in the future.

No. 5 Month

This month is a period of change and adjustment, though only for a short time. The home situation may go through minor changes. Your employment situation may improve provided you are ready to be advanced. This can be accomplished by the wise use of words while dealing with higher authorities.

No. 6 Month

This cycle is the embodiment of the laws of material supply and education. For this reason, this month is one in which you will not have to worry particularly about the source of your income. However, you may have to share it, for the law of education implies the necessity of learning the lesson of unselfishness and accepting your responsibilities. Try to enhance the beauty of your surroundings, for the vibrations are favourable for the increase of enjoyment through the decorative arts. While you will have to adopt a realistic and adult attitude towards your tasks and duties, you will also have the pleasure to be gained from a feeling of confidence and a deep sense of appreciation of all that is lovely in nature and in art.

No. 7 Month

The more serious aspects of life will probably have a stronger appeal for you this month than will the frivolous or temporary pleasures. You can now study yourself, your friends, and your environment with a detachment that is cool and clear. Be grateful for this change to see things as they are, for it gives you the opportunity to evaluate that which does not exist when you are in an emotional mood. Be prepared to cast off the implements of life that are not worth your while. Make the decision to study, and let your field of study be broad. Life itself as well as its population and customs are as valuable fields of investigation as the arts and crafts, not to say vocational subjects. Mystic studies should also attract you during this month, and you should have some marked degree of success in the investigation of the hidden side of nature.

No. 8 Month

Power and energy are yours during the month when the 8 vibration reigns. This is a cycle in which you should assume the direction of all the affairs with which you are connected. All business deals should follow the pattern that you design, whether you are a tycoon or just a housewife who does the daily marketing. Play the role of the director, for this is your cosmic function under the present influence. Make achievement your aim of the month; now is the time to show the world (as well as yourself) that you have the determination to fulfil every one of your potentialities. Do not forget the plight of those less fortunate than yourself during this time of success and prosperity. It is truly more blessed to give than to receive and this blessing may be yours this month.

No. 9 Month

This is an excellent month if you use its numerical vibration for the correct purpose, and that is to get rid of old habits of thought and action that are deterring your progress. Keep in communication with persons who are far away, as this may lead to an unexpected opportunity. Spend at least a part of the time in the study of occult subjects, for the number 9 rules the study of the mysteries behind the veil. You may have surprising psychic experiences, and your intuition should surely be very keen. Do not seek outside advice, for the answer to your immediate problems lies within yourself. Consider this as a period set aside for casting off the useless and preparing to begin anew. Face the next cycle with optimism and confidence.

CHAPTER 21

HOW IS THIS YEAR FOR YOU!

It is a very simple matter to calculate your individual year. What you have to do is to add the date and the month to the current year. In our last example we took your birth-date as 14-9-1962. In order to compute a particular year for you, we have not to take into consideration the year of your birth i.e. 1962. Instead we have to take the current year about which we want to know:

This can be worked out as under:

Date of your birth	14
Month of your birth	9
Current year	1989
	2012

Now reduce the above total to a single digit which comes to 5. Thus the year 1989 would be a 5 individual year cycle. Please read the explanation given to number 5.

In this way you have to calculate each year you want to know about. The significance from number 1 to 9 would be as under:

No. 1 Year

The coming year holds out hopes of large scale improvement in many directions. You will at last be able to take the lead and shape your circumstances to your betterment. You will be more egotistical and you have to be on your guard against being too selfish. You also have to think twice before you allow your pride to stand in your way; otherwise it will prove very expensive. If you are holding a key position in your job, you will show great interest in your activities whereby you will benefit a lot. Do not be afraid of asking favours from your superiors. This is the year when you will derive much benefit through influence. As fortunate developments in this year grow, you will increase your self-confidence. You will find yourself becoming a centre of activities and in a position to enhance your prestige and social status. You will find others in your circle more responsive to your leadership. Look therefore for greater power, fresh opportunities, but do not be surprised if responsibilities grow heavier. Your new associates will become your lasting friends.

No. 2 Year

This is the year of romance which will help to lighten your burden and give added interest to your daily routine. In this year you will get an opportunity for gaining information which would be helpful to you in later years. There will be slow progress in realising your ambition and you will gradually change the direction of your efforts as you will have fresh ideas and outlets. You will develop a more imaginative temperament which may help your romantic event this year. Sentiments too will have free play. Close relatives will have great influence over important new trends. There is likely to be some development in connection with someone living abroad.

Your magnetism will attract new friends and a receptive attitude will bring you much more than an aggressive one. Do not be impatient; please wait and watch. Partnerships which will prosper are also indicated. It is wiser to work out minor aspects than to launch big, new projects at this time. Important matters on the emotional plane may be exaggerated. You may find it difficult to maintain an even balance in your relations with older people or parents. In general, this will be a good year for you.

No. 3 Year

This is the year of success. Yet you should not consider this year merely lucky because the negative aspects of the number 3 tends to scatter your interests in many fields. Self-expression is in prominence this year and so you should be careful of what you say. You can market your ideas through words, story, play, or script. The coming year will be more expansive than you have experienced for the last 6 or 7 years. There are signs of an increase in your financial earnings and of development of more cheerful and optimistic outlook. Your intimate partners will be helpful and sympathetic as per your wish.

A more calm and collected behaviour will be cultivated. Your former depression and pessimism will be entirely replaced and you will begin to look for higher progress.

No. 4 Year

This is a notable year. There will be number of changes and an atmosphere of unsettlement. Unexpected and sudden developments will take place and these will involve forming several new association and friendships. However, do not consider this year as one of negative tension. You may expect a series of lucky incidents this year. You are likely to undertake original and rather speculative tasks because these are likely to prove most advantageous. Your outlook will become more unconventional. You will place great weight on new attachments, and puzzle your partners by an increasing tendency to make sudden changes without warning.

The symbol of the number 4 is a square, within which you are standing. Naturally this restricts you as far as expansion is concerned. However, this does not prevent you from growing in an upward direction.

No. 5 Year

No. 5 Vibrations come under the rulership of Mercury. This year, therefore, is a pleasant year for you. There will be travels either for business or pleasure. During this year you will discover the power of your elegance to sway audiences. The period is favourable for lecturing, teaching, writing, dramatics, and all communications through advertising, and over the telephone and the postal service. You will be busy in intellectual pursuits in study, reading, music and theatrical activities.

Throughout the year you will be fully occupied with your commercial undertakings. Buying, selling and bargaining will play a larger role and there is also the prospect of increased travel. You are sure to receive some fresh offers which hold the possibility of an improvement in your status. There will be a new agreement entered into with someone and this document is sure to have a far-reaching influence over your material affairs. Temperamentally you will be more uneasy and uncertain. A worrying, nervous complex will need to be checked.

No. 6 Year

This is a year of social contacts and friendly atmosphere. Much greater attention will be paid to your home and family life. Your friends and partners can be influenced but they will be quite slow to respond to strong handed tactis. You will develop a more easy-going attitude. The outlook will be more cheerful and will have greater influence over your decisions.

Whether you are at home or away from home during this year, your mind will be occupied by domestic matters. You are likely to assume responsibilities of your family and you will find it difficult to balance the budget. Married life will be happy and harmonious in this year. Comfort and culture in your surroundings should fall a perfect blend of the intellectual and the emotional aspects of your life.

No. 7 Year

This is the year of peace. This should be easily accomplished because the number 7 is intellectual by nature and should stimulate your mental potentialities. Your affairs will move slowly. Matters related to distance should be attended to immediately so that good fortune may lie in that direction. Keep your correspondence with friends and relatives who are far way. If you are starting on a career, it would be well to choose one dealing with travel or communication.

There are possibilities that you will be misrepresented or misunderstood over an important matter and it will be extremely difficult to make your point of view clear. Your temperament will be conditioned by a more positive type of person who will have much to do with your life. Your mind will be more imaginative but you will also be increasingly moody.

No. 8 Year

The shadow of the past is sure to exert a heavy influence over the coming year. The older members of society are likely to have dominance in your decisions this year. Do not look for quick results. All the indications point to a slow moving, rather ponderous trend with recurring delays and frustrations. You may get opportunities for extra responsibilities to organise your affairs on a better footing. Some gain will accrue through buying but it is not a favourable time to sell. Investment in insurance and government securities will prove more prudent than quick profit speculations.

Energy and force are bestowed upon you during this year. You should use this power in a creative and constructive way. All your executive powers are to the fore this year and you should be able to command any situation. Your greatest reward may come to you in the form of the satisfaction you get from knowing that your conduct is ethical and that you are making an effort to improve not only yourself but mankind as well.

No. 9 Year

You may expect a variety of experiences this year. The number 9 represents the closing of a nine year cycle and this indicates the end of one type of living and the beginning of another with renewed hope and enthusiasm. Your psychological attitude towards this year is very important. You should cultivate the attitude that all things come to an end—but to make way for the new. You will experience this year that you can rely confidently upon your impressions. The number 9 is the ruler of occultism and this is a propitious year in which to further your studies along these lines. Take advantage of the positive type, to acquire all the culture, knowledge and appreciation of the arts that the number 9 favours.

This year will be more dashing and aggressive. The result will lead to a stiff battle with fate, but the odds are on you. Be on your guard not to involve in quarrels. The general undertone of impatience is sure to provoke friction and you will be involved in disputes. The more pushful and go ahead of your companions will have a greater influence over your life. It would be better to listen to them so that you will get many useful hints and information from them. You will become much more impulsive, reckless and ambitious. Speech will be more direct, emphatic and candid.

Thus we have completed the significance of your year cycle.

CHAPTER 22

THE DAY OF YOUR BIRTH

Day Of The Week From The Birth-Date

It is an interesting calculation to find out the day of the week from the complete date of birth. It is equally interesting to know that during your discussions with your client you can astonish him by telling him his day of birth. You can do so by secretly doing some calculations from the complete date of birth of your client. This secret formula is as under:

There are certain numbers allotted to each month and to centuries. Numbers allotted to centuries are as under:

18th Century	No. 4
19th Century	No. 2
20th Century	No. 0
21st Century	No. 6

The numbers allotted to individual months are as under:

January	No. 1
February	No. 4
March	No. 4
April	No. 0
May	No. 2
June	No. 5
July	No. 0
August	No. 3
September	No. 6

October	No. 1
November	No. 4
December	No. 6

In leap years, numbers to January and February are 0 and 3 respectively.

Let us take a birth date, 16-8-1960.

1. We have to divide the last two digits of the century by 4. Thus 60 ÷ 4 = 15
2. Add this figure of 15 to the year of birth i.e. 60. Thus 60 + 15 = 75
3. Add the date of birth to the above figure of 75. 16 + 75 = 91
4. Add the number allotted to the month of birth. 3 + 91 = 94
5. Add the number allotted to the 20th Century which is 0.

Now divide this figure of 94 by 7 and find out the remainder. The remainder is 3 and therefore the day is Tuesday. The relation between the remainder and the day of the week is as under:

If the remainder is 0, it is Saturday

If the remainder is 1, it is Sunday

If the remainder is 2, it is Monday

If the remainder is 3, it is Tuesday

If the remainder is 4, it is Wednesday

If the remainder is 5, it is Thursday

If the remainder is 6, it is Friday

In the above birth date, 16-8-1960, we notify that it is a leap ,year and if the month of birth is January or February instead of August, the month number will be 0 or 3.

The day of the week also has its ruling planet which also affects the behaviour of the person.

There are seven days of the week and each day is dominated by a particular planet as under:

Day	Planet	Ruling No.
Sunday	Sun	1
Monday	Moon	2 and 7
Tuesday	Mars	9
Wednesday	Mercury	5
Thursday	Jupiter	3
Friday	Venus	6
Saturday	Saturn	8 and 4

In our study of the Ruling Numbers, we have allotted No. 7 to Neptune and No. 4 to Uranus. But since these two planets do not have their individual days and since they have similar characteristics to the planets Moon and Saturn, their numbers 7 and 4 are allotted to Moon and Saturn respectively.

If your Ruling Number is 1 and also you are born on Sunday, you definitely acquire the characteristics of the planet Sun. But in case your Ruling Number is 1 but you are born on Monday, then you have combined characteristics of the planets Sun and Moon and so on. Thus while explaining the characteristics of a person, do not forget to take into account the planet allotted to the day on which the person is born.

CHAPTER 23

TRACING OUT THINGS LOST

Theory

Everyone has a conscious mind and a subconscious mind. Modern science is investigating the function of the subconscious mind. It has discovered that this has a tremendous potential and a power which can often show wonderful results. Every brain, while functioning, creates definite vibrations or waves in the ethereal atmosphere. These waves impinge upon the brains of others and cause a perception of personality so that the individuals affected will immediately create a mental image of the person whose thought is projected and whose presence is shortly made apparent to the senses. However, in this process the transmitter is wholly unaware of the fact that his thought waves have an effect on the subconscious of the other person. This process takes place on the level of the subconscious of the two persons. A conclusion, based upon a close study of this familiar but little understood phenomenon, is that the subconscious of the projector is not only aware of the presence of other minds, but is capable of projecting itself into immediate relations with them. This projection is received by the subconscious mind of the other person and later on received by the conscious mind. Extremely sensitive persons not only receive the waves but also a vision.

This subconscious mind has an ability to peep into the future and can register future events well in advance. Based on this theory and assumption, it is inferred that the mind can give out certain numbers which can be interpreted to locate the place where a lost article can be found.

A person who has lost his article is asked to utter any 9 numbers one after another. The numbers should come spontaneously. These nine numbers are totalled up and 3 is added in the total. The total is referred to in the nature of the question.

Example: The nine numbers given at random are set as under:

967487942 = 56 + 3 = 59

The interpretation of number 59 is then referred to the chart. The answer is "It is in a flour or powder required for cooking". The meaning of various numbers is as follows. If the result is:

1 The article may be in the living room near a white curtain. A smart child may know it.

2 It is near some utensil and a servant may be helpful.

3 Amongst books or papers or in a passage.

4 It is actually misplaced and not lost.

5 Try for it under a cloak or garment or on a hook for hanging clothes.

6 Near the footwear.

7 A female member of the family has kept it while arranging clothes.

8 On the top of a cupboard or a shelf. Take the help of an assistant.

9 In the robes or clothing of young ones.

10 It is in the drawing room, you will get it back.

11 It is near a water place, but not in the house but at some distance. Think of a picnic spot you recently visited.

12 The article is safe. Search for it at your working place.

13 Search for it in your cloak room or on the hanger.

14 You may not recover the article. Anyway search the cleaning place.

15 Somewhere near where the animals (cow, horses, dogs) are kept. Enquire of your spouse.

16 You can get it. Contact your cook.

17 Near the important securities and on the shelf.

18 It is in the house itself and hidden in clothes.

19 In a small passage or lane slightly away from the house.

20 It is only misplaced. Search near water or the carpet.

21 It is in a trunk, suit-case or a box.

22 It is at a height within the house. May be on a shelf.

23 It is in the wardrobe or among washing clothes.

24 It is safe and will be found in due course.

25 Be quick to search for it among your articles.

26 It might be in a very safe place. Contact elder members.

27 Ask the car driver or search for it in the garage.

28 Forget about getting back the article. It is totally lost.

29 It has been given to someone. It will be returned to you.

30 It was lost during the play time children. Contact them.

31 Don't worry. It is near the bath room or washing place.

32 It is in the passage or a corridor or a closed place.

33 It is hidden in your clothes.

34 You may get it near the cooking gas or a fire-place.

35 It may be near the attached bath.

36 You will get it through your servant.

37 It is lying on the floor in your room.

38 It is near the swimming tank.

39 It is on a shelf.

40 By chance it has been wrapped in your clothes.

41 Near the footwear.

42 It is near water or in the premises of the servant.

43 Search for it near the garage.

44 It is near the oil containers.

45 It is on the cupboard or on a shelf.

46 Ask your partner.

47 One of your servants has committed the theft.

48 It is near the drinking water.

49 You will not get it.

50 It is in a box, suitcase or a trunk.

51 It is near your bathing place.

52 Enquire with the mistress of the house or her relatives. It has changed hands.

53 A person who is in possession of the article will return it.

54 Search where the children play.

55 It is near a water draining place.

56 It is where you last halted.

57 It may be in your playing kit.

58 It is very difficult to get it back. Two persons have got hold of it.

59 It is in flour or powder required for cooking. Ask the senior servant.

60 You can forget about it. It is lost for ever.

61 It is near a wall.

62 It is very difficult to trace it.

63 It may be in the lumber room.

64 It is not lost. Search for it in dark corners.

65 Chances of getting it back are poor.

66 It has been stolen by two servants who have conspired together. A slightly handicapped servant may be questioned. But there is little possibility of recovery.

67 A boy in the family will assist you in the matter.

68 Ask someone to collect it from the top of the house.

69 It may be at the entrance of the house of your relative or at a place you last visited.

70 It is near a water place.

71 Search for it on the floor near your feet.

72 It is near a water reservoir.

73 You will have to lodge a regular complaint about the theft with the police.

74 It will be found by a careful servant.

75 Youngsters have taken it and it will be returned in a damaged condition.

76 It is near some food.

77 A servant in the house will fetch it for you.

78 Very difficult to recover.

79 Search near the iron cupboard.

80 It is in a box, trunk or a case.

81 You will be lucky to find it in your clothes.

82 You will get it in the kitchen.

83 A young girl will recover it from a water tank.

84 It is in a box or a case.

We can find out things lost by another system also which is known as the *pyramid system.* See Chapter 24.

CHAPTER 24

THE PYRAMID SYSTEM

The Pyramid system in the field of numerology is another wonder of the psychic phenomenon. As stated in an earlier chapter, man is gifted with psychic powers which are of various kinds and we must know how to tap those powers. In the study of numerology there is a vast scope for the use of these psychic powers in daily life. With the help of the Pyramid System, any question can be solved with great accuracy. However there are three important conditions:

1. The questioner should be sincere.

2. His difficulty should be real and honest.

3. He should put up his difficulty spontaneously.

The same question is not to be repeated again. If we try to play mischief with this system, the answers and results will be wrong and misleading. In nature there are symbols which have their own laws and functions but which are wholly unintelligible to the modern world. Our ancient scholars were master of occult powers and they discovered the hidden meaning of these symbols in nature. The Pyramid System is also the outcome of their discoveries.

Taking it for granted that the person who approaches us for consultation is sincere about his difficulty, and his difficulty is genuine, he should be requested to ask his question in a spontaneous manner. The words should come naturally, without much thought.

After such a question is put, the number of the words is counted and set down. This figure is followed by the number of letters in each of the words, and the line is completed. The figures in this line are then successively added together, the first with second, the second with the third, the third with the fourth, and so on until they have been paired and added. This addition is reduced to a single digit if it exceeds 9, and then written in the second line and in between the two numbers which have been added. These are then treated in the same manner by successive pairing and addition and a third line is produced. Since each successive line is one figure less than the one above it, it follows that the process eventually tapers to a single figure. It is this figure that is referred to as its planetary equivalent and the interpretation made thence in accordance with the nature of the question. Let us take an example.

A student asks, "Shall I get through my examination".

There are 6 words in this sentence, so the figure 6 is set down first. "Shall" contains 5 letters, therefore the figure 5 follows the figure 6; "I" is 1; "get" is 3; "through" is 7; "my" is 2 and lastly the word "examination" contains 11 letters; i.e. 2.

If we arrange these figures one after another, the first line stands thus:

6 5 1 3 7 2 2

The Pyramid when completed will be as follows:

6 5 1 3 7 2 2
2 6 4 1 9 4
8 1 5 1 4
9 6 6 5
6 3 2
9 5
5

The resultant figure is 5 which is the number of Mercury. It is concerned with education and therefore, the boy would get through this examination.

(1) If the resultant is 1 it shows success.

(2) If the resultant is 2, it is concerned with the planet Moon which shows lack of concentration and uneasiness. However the Moon is associated with liquids and if the subject is medicine, pathology or chemistry, he will get through.

(3) If the resultant is 3, it represents Jupiter which is a good plane showing ambition. We can conclude that the student may get through his exam and further his ambitions.

(4) If the resultant is 4, it represents the planet Uranus, which shows upheavals and uncertainties, so there is no guarantee.

(5) If the resultant is 5, we have seen above that he will get through.

(6) If the resultant is 6, it represents Venus. If the study course is in arts, the student will get through. But if the study course is in science, then there are few hopes of his getting through.

(7) If the resultant is 7, it represents Neptune and engineering or electronic subjects. If the student is appearing for these subjects, he will get through.

(8) If the resultant is 8, it represents Saturn and shows delays and difficulties. We can predict uncertainty.

(9) If the resultant is 9, it represents Mars which shows dash and courage and is associated with military or engineering subjects. On the strength of his dashing nature and confidence, he may get through his examination.

In the Pyramid System, the interpretation also should be spontaneous. It should come out immediately. However, in order to get a correct interpretation of the number, it is necessary to be conversant with all the qualities of that number.

Sometimes it is also useful to note whether the resultant number is odd or even. As stated in the introduction, according to the Chinese system and also the Pythagorean System, odd numbers are positive, energetic, mainly, showing heat and fire, whereas even numbers denote a female, darkness, coldness and are of ephemeral value. Supposing a woman expecting a child shortly asks whether she will have a son or a daughter, and the resultant number is odd, the answer is a son and if the resultant number is even, the answer is a daughter. Thus we have to use this Pyramid System very intelligently and our intuition has to play a role in it.

CHAPTER 25

HORSE RACING

It is difficult to find an individual who is not interested in getting a windfall or getting rich in one night. Everybody is interested in lottery, horse racing, casino and such other sports or games whereby he would get rich without effort. Horse racing is one of the avenues which has been an attraction to millions of people all over the world.

There are various systems or methods with the help of which a winner in a horse race is worked out. People take into consideration the age of the horse, his previous record, the handicap he has got, his weight, the length of the race, the jockey who is to ride him and so on and so forth. Numerology is one of the simplest methods to work out the horse which will achieve success and bring money. The method of finding out one's lucky horse is as under:

1. The person should always try only his lucky number. If he is born on the 1st, 10th, 19th or 28th of any month, his lucky number is 1 and he is governed by the planet Sun. Number 4 is the counterpart of number 1 and therefore this person should always try those horses whose serial numbers are 1 and 4.

2. Every number has its lucky colours. The Jockeys wear caps of different colours and the person should find out a jockey who is wearing a cap of his lucky colour.

We have now to combine the number of the horse and the lucky colour. The lucky colours of number 1 person are yellow, orange and gold. If the jockey is wearing a cap having one of these colours, well and good. If the colours are different but of those of number 4, the person can try horse number 1 because number 4 is equally lucky for him.

If the colour of the cap is not in harmony with the lucky number, the person should see whether the horse is a favourite or a fluke. If the horse is a favourite and the colour is lucky, it is advisable to try on that horse.

3. We should work out the mental vibrations (vowels) of the name of the horse and the name of the jockey. If these vibrations are in harmony with our name vibrations, we try that horse or that jockey which is favourable to us. It is also useful if their vibrations and those indicated by numbers favourable for marriage are in harmony.

From the above, it is clear that before we select the horse we have to think of:

a. our lucky number,

b. lucky colour,

c. name of the horse,

d. name of the jockey,

e. the colour of jockey's cap,

f. our lucky number for marriage,

g. whether the horse is a fluke or favourite.

After taking all these factors, and their combinations into consideration, we have to make the final selection of the winning horse.

It is my experience of several years based on statistical data that horses with numbers 3 or 6 usually win in the 3rd or the 6th race. That horse with No. 3 or No. 6 will be either *win* or *placed* in the 3rd race and also in the 6th race.

It is therefore advisable that in the 3rd race, you should place your bet on two horses, No. 3 and No. 6 Either of the horses will be either win or place. Similarly in the 6th race, you should try No. 3 and No. 6. Your horse will be either win or place.

I request horse racing lovers, to try this method and inform me of their results.

CHAPTER 26

THOUGHT READING

You have seen in Chapter 23, 'Tracing out things lost' that the human mind has tremendous power to penetrate the future. The human brain is a store of such powers and the ancient Yogis, by their peace, mediation and sadhana (continuous process of study), had discovered that certain powers can be acquired and developed by practising a particular type of meditation. In our 'Patanjali Yoga Sutras', in the third part 'Vibhuti Pad', the sage Patanjali has mentioned several types of meditations whereby we can attain certain siddhies (mastery) and fulfil our wishes. In Tibet also, monks have developed different sadhanas for accomplishing certain Siddhies. The Hindu technique and the Tibetan technique may be different but the results are the same. Meditation is a process of thought and by our concentrating on a particular thought, we develop the power of our mind in such a way that we achieve our end through the process of that meditation.

Theory

There are thousands of centres in the brain, each having innumerable powers. If these centres are stimulated, they exhibit their powers. The ancient sages knew the powers of different brain centres and they also knew very well how to stimulate those centres. They therefore discovered different types of meditations whereby the desired centres of the brain could be stimulated and the person would acquire powers ascribed to that centre. As a part of logic, we may say that if any of these brain centres be located and if that centre be stimulated artificially, the person may acquire the power of that centre. It is the province of modern science to investigate the matter.

Experience

1. Once a friend of mine, who was a big dignitary in the Central Government of India, narrated his experience in Sikkim, a province on the North-East border of India. One day, at about 12 noon he was walking on a road below a hill when a person walked down the hill and told my friend that the Lama desired to take his lunch with my friend. My friend accepted the invitation and started climbing the hill by the small road. His guide walked at a distance of about five feet away from my friend, but two feet above the ground. When they reached the top of the hill they entered the abode of the Lama. My friend had a meeting with the lama and after sometime they went to lunch. The Lama sat on the side of the dining table opposite my friend. It was a matter of great surprise to my friend that he could see that Lama through and through. During their discussions, the Lama told my friend that what they were talking about was "the level of words", whereas when he talked with the other Lamas, it was on "the level of thought". When they talked "on the level of Thought", there were no barriers and they could talk with each other thousands of miles apart.

2. A certain person known as Messing had the power of reading the thoughts of others. In 1927 he visited India and exhibited his powers to Mahatma Gandhi. He informed Mahatmajee that he would act as per the thoughts of Mahatmajee. Mahatma Gandhi just thought to himself that the exhibitor Mr. Messing should take the flute (a musical instrument) which was in the window and should carry it to the next room and hand it over to one Mr. Ghosh. No sooner

Mahatmajee thought of this, than Mr. Messing acted upon his instructions (given mentally by Mahatmajee) and handed the flute to Mr. Ghosh.

This Mr. Messing also demonstrated his thought reading powers to Mr. Stalin, the President of the U.S.S.R Mr. Stalin mentally thought of certain orders which were instantly obeyed by Mr. Messing.

3. As against the above Mr. Messing, there was another person called Mr. Malencov. He had the ability to transmit his thoughts and force them on others. When the Russian Scientist Mr. Pavlov came to know of this, he called Mr. Malencov and conducted few experiments. He asked Mr. Malencov to sit in a room in Moscow and give him a 'lock'. He was asked to transmit the thought of the "lock" to another person, 300 miles away and in Leningard. The instrument "E.E.G." (Electroencephelogram) was attached to the head of Mr. Malencov and also to the other person sitting 300 miles away.

As Mr. Malenclov started transmitting his thoughts, the E.E.G. machine on his head started showing the thought waves, and surprisingly, similar waves were noticed on the E.E.G. machine attached to the other person. After Mr. Malenclov completed his thought transmission, of the "Lock" before him, the other person in Leningard could describe the article and finally identified it as the "Lock".

4. I will now narrate one more experience from my own life and then proceed with our theory of Numerology.

It was in 1970 that once two of my friends had come to my place for discussions. During our discussions, the atmosphere in my room changed and a stage came when three of us could communicate to each other on the "level of thought", without uttering a single word. We exchanged thoughts but without speech. However, this atmosphere remained for a few minutes only and again we continued our talks.

I have described above the power of the mind and how thoughts could be transmitted or could be received. We sometimes say "Think of the Devil and the Devil stands before you." This is a common phenomenon in every day life. While walking down a street, we think of a person and we meet him on the next corner. (An instance of Telepathy).

The thought waves are capable of numerical expression. In order to find out the thought of an individual, the following procedure is to be adopted.

The person whose thought is to be read, has to speak out 9 numbers spontaneously as they occur. All the 9 numbers are totalled up and 3 is added to the total. You have to look to the significance given to the total thus arrived at.

The process employed is based upon the occult fact that, if the mind is concerned about any matter, the figures that are then automatically delivered by the mind bear a direct relationship to the nature of the thought, and in themselves afford the means of a solution. An instance of this may be cited from the scripture, which the Cabalists have revealed. In the prophecy of Jacob concerning the future of his sons, Judah is referred to as a lion's whelp. 'The sceptre shall not depart from Judah, nor the law-giver from between his feet, until Shiloh shall come." The sceptre is Regulus, the law giver is Cepheus, and Shiloh or Shuleh is Cor Scorpio.

Example: What am I thinking of?

985627142	=	44
Add		3
		47

The answer: "You are thinking of a value, measure, or weight, a matter of proportion, and of yourself in certain relations."

Things Thought Of

The significance of numbers is as under:

1 You think of position, of elevation, things above you, a master or progenitor, a pinnacle, head, or prominence, and its levelling or downfall.

2 Of distance, things remote, a journey or a foreign land.

3 You think of a personal event, an ailment, probably a fever, heat or anger.

4 Of a domestic affair. The family circle, love and pleasure; of the heart, or something greatly desired.

5 Of marriage; and understanding or agreement; of things in union or harmony.

6 Of news, things related, a brother, means of communication, journeys.

7 Of a house, of things underground, of a land or water in expense or the ocean, change or removal.

8 Of antique things or foreign products, a foreign country, of the Orient.

9 Of a death or loss, of defective contracts of means of restitution.

10 Of an unfortunate alliance, troublesome agreement, or disputation.

11 Of the value of property, a mine, or matter relating to real estate.

12 Of pleasant surroundings, some festivity, gala, convivial meeting, fine clothes and personal comforts.

13 Of money, speculative matters, gain.

14 Of a short journey, a cruise, or matters connected with messages across the water; a female relation.

15 Of a bereavement or death; funeral vestments, mourning; a loss or misfortune.

16 Of a fortunate and happy alliance, a wife, a good understanding or agreement.

17 Of a servant; or nearer to yourself, of some discomfort, disease or ailment.

18 Of a pleasant journey, a thing of gold; love; domesticity of joy; a brother, or a message desired.

19 Of some restraint, confinement, imprisonment, seclusion; a child.

20 Of a journey or letter; something carried; yourself in communication with another, a roadway.

21 Of gain, money, some financial advantage, things in possession, of something white and silvery, a rupee.

22 Of an unfortunate marriage or a sick partner, a bad contract, difficulties, an enemy or rival.

23 Of good living, rich clothes, plentiful food, faithful servants good health, creature comforts, position.

24 Of uncertain position, a family dispute; children, an unfortunate venture; illicit love affairs.

25 Of much gain, great wealth, gold, the sun, something shining or brilliance.

26 Of peaceful possession, good property, the house, of level ground, foundations.

27 A closed place or room, a short journey by boat; of a brother, or person in relation to yourself, a letter or a messenger.

28 Of yourself in imagination; of white linen; a bowl or silver pot; a new moon.

29 Of ill-health; a blood disorder; poor fare; a time of poverty and trial.

30 Of happy children, a pleasant experience, union, a fortunate dowry or legacy.

31 Of something underground, a snake in the house, a scorpion or reptile, a foreign land.

32 Of a king or rajah, a golden vestment, the sun, your own individuality and character.

33 Of a pleasant message, a good position, a brother, some distinction.

34 Of financial benefit, a purchase of food or other necessities, grain etc. some corporeal benefit.

35 Of a female, a birth, a plot or scheme, something secret to yourself; a confinement.

36 Of a loss by speculation, a sick child, an unhappy family, misery and trouble.

37 Of an unfortunate contract, an unhappy marriage, a house or property, a stable.

38 Of a death by malaria or enteric fever; of a journey, a message; of a sister; a neighboring tank or pool.

39 Of a closed place or temple; a gilded chamber, a king's sequestration or exile.

40 Of money, things of value, jewels or apparel, the price of grain.

41 Of yourself or your figure, your apparel, investiture, food, position, credit.

42 Of a friend, a woman of quality, a patroness or her favour, a gathering of people, a convention.

43 Of ancestral property, an old man, an old building, the value of minerals, a cemetery.

44 Of a brother, a letter from across the seas or from a great distance, a book of theology, a sastra, of good health, of personal comforts, a luxury.

45 Of a marriage, of gain or loss, a thing of small value, a paisa, tilt, bias, inequality, fraud.

46 Of a friend, a man of position and honour; something of gold, of value, a jewel, a ring of gold.

47 Of yourself, of justice, of equity, of value, measure, weight, proportion, peace, satisfaction, rest, a death.

48 Of a robing-room, a private place, a servant in hiding, woman's health, of news from a distance.

49 Of a change of position, your own mother, a thing of distinction, a capitol, a woman in power, a queen or rani.

50 Of a painful journey, a sister in distress, a doleful message, a call to office.

51 Of gain and affluence, a stake or bet, of children, money from afar, a profession.

52 Of personal disease or death, things lost, hidden, or occult, of a man servant; a red cloth; hot food; a doctor; yama; a reptile.

53 Of high office, the rajah or king, a man in power, loss of gold, a dead lion.

54 Of a dangerous illness, a woman in distress, of a wife, a girl, a contract or agreement, four walls.

55 Of a death, a lost paper, a message gone astray, a young girl, a gathering, a friend.

56 Of a foreign country beyond the seas, of a sea voyage, a s'akti, a religious gathering, a publication, a ship, a ghost.

57 Of acquired wealth, a board or store, a pension or inheritance, a male relative.

58 Of acquisition, personal influence, a grandee, vakil or lawyer, a judge, guru or purohita, instruction, the Vedas, a Brahmin; personal property, estate.

59 Of a death-chamber, a hospital or sick room, a male child; the household fire, a venture or hazard.

60 Of a Parsee, a religious ceremony; a foreign king, a rishi; samadhi, Brahma; the sun of heaven; Ishvara; time.

61 Of food; trading; fine apparel; a male friend; a market-place or exchange; a manservant; a vaishnavite Brahmin.

62 Of a writing or agreement; an undertaking or contract; a legal process; position; mastership, a father.

63 Of a dead woman; some lost property; a winding-sheet or death-cloth; a waning moon; the wife's dowry; an ablution.

64 Of yourself in regard to position; of acquired property, an inheritance; an old man; duration; a bargain or exchange.

65 Of a short journey and return; going and coming; a journey on foot; a closed room; a fortunate confinement; a sister; a mantram.

66 A smashana or burning ground; a rocky place; minerals; a medical adviser; a dead friend; a burning house; dry ground or sand.

67 A dead Rajah; the loss of gold; the wife's dowry; a girdle; a sick child.

68 Of a female child; the home circle; a position of trust; security.

69 Of clothing; a servant; a ship; merchandise; foodstuffs; trade; a thing of science; a vedanga.

70 Of a wife; an agreement; a public gathering; a full moon.

71 A waterpot or kumbha; an old association; a friend; yourself with others in company; a private place or room; a warder.

72 Of wealth; a princely friend; a Brahmin; a religious meeting; of sandals and things in pairs.

73 Of a brother; a position; the death of a ruler; a quick journey an angry message; honours; succession; a writing.

74 Of a brilliant sun; a great shining; eyesight; a proud wife; a powerful enemy, hunting.

75 Of a pleasant place; a rich estate; moksha; buried treasure; cattle.

76 Of a son; a place of learning; a school-house, a bridge; a Bramhachari (ascetic).

77 Of a white turban or dhoti; a serving maid; medicine; water; drinking.

78 Of an aged friend; an institution; an old alliance; a hospital; a man in prison.

79 Of oneself; of increase and prosperity, position, power, and affluence; of extremities, the feet; a pair of sandals; an understanding; a judge or advocate.

80 Of gain; a risk of loss; a loss by fire; of a foreign land; a far off death; a pralaya (deluge); a voyage.

81 Of a rich relative; fine apparel; gold ornaments; personal health; ripe fruit.

82 Of a peaceful death; a rich dowry; a pleasant message; an elephant ride; a journey for profit; a sister.

83 Of trading; a treaty or agreement; a lease of property; a gateway or; passage; a bride or betrothal.

84 Of a daughter; a tank or bathing place; a public festival; Durga; a holiday; clean linen; or a beloved.

At this point the enumerations cease, since there are numbers employed and none can be more than 9, so that $9^2 + 3 = 84$ will complete the resolutions. There are, it will be observed, several interpretations to each resultant number, but when the kabala is worked out to its finality, there is little doubt as to which interpretation to use.

CHAPTER 27

ALL ABOUT YOUR MARRIAGE

You have studied how to make a choice of your life partner in the chapter dealing with your Ruling Number and also the month you are born in. You shall now study it in slightly greater detail.

As you know, marriage is a complicated structure made up of a whole series of subjective and objective factors of a heterogeneous nature. Therefore, when the question of marriage is considered, factors of importance to be taken note of are physical fitness, sexual compatibility, temperamental qualities and social and economic status; so that the relations between the couple may stand the strain of maladjustments.

Astrology has developed its own methods for marriage compatibility which have been in vogue from time immemorial. From the study of palms also, you can find out whether the two individuals who intend to come together have a natural compatibility.

The study of numerology will also be a good guide in this respect as it will help the two individuals to understand each other in a better way. As has been stressed all the time, this study helps in psycho-analysis. It is absolutely necessary for a married couple to understand each other's approach towards life and also the abilities, capacities, likes and dislikes. In the absence of this understanding, there is hardly any possibility that the two can stay together happily.

To start your study, let us suppose that your date of birth is 14th September 1948. From this birth date you have to find out towards whom you have a natural affinity, who are your friends and who can be your life partner. In the matter you will have to refer to your individual Ruling Number and also to your month of birth. You have to refer to the Summary Charts given at the end of Chapter 12 and also Chapter 13. In both these chapters you have to refer to the column 'Marriage Partner'. Now we have presumed your birth-date as 24th, i.e. you have to refer to the Ruling Number 6 and the column 'Marriage';

In the above column the period given is:

21st August to 20th September

21st December to 20th January.

The above period shows your natural affinity. So basically you can select a partner from the above period. The Ruling Numbers 2, 3, 6 and 9 are given. That means all those who have these Ruling Numbers have compatibility with you. You have now to combine the favourable dates (Ruling Numbers) and the period. You have to select the dates in the favourable period and the result is as under:

Dates in August:
21st, 24th, 29th, 30th.

Dates in September:
2nd, 3rd, 6th, 11th, 12th, 15th, 20th.

Dates in December:
21st, 24th, 29th, 30th.

Dates in January:
2nd, 3rd, 6th, 11th, 12th, 15th, 20th.

Your birth month is Septembers please refer to the chart for the months and find out the period and the dates for marriage compatibility. You will find that the period is the same as studied above but there is a variation in the Ruling Numbers. So you can positively select your partner born on the dates and in the above period. If however, there is no common factor between the period according to the Ruling Number and according to the month you are born in, then go by the Ruling Number only.

How To Find Out The Year Of Marriage:

Many a time the parents of a daughter or a son may approach you to enquire about the year of marriage of their daughter. During my study of this subject for over 40 years, I have collected certain data regarding the date of birth and the year of marriage. After tabulating several such birth dates I have arrived at the conclusion that atleast in about 40% cases there is a relation between the Ruling Number and the year of marriage. The method is as under:

The relation between the Ruling Number (date of the month) and the year of marriage is as under:

Ruling No.	*Year of Marriage*
1	1, 4, 5, 7
2	1, 5, 6, 8
3	3, 6, 7, 9
4	1, 4, 7, 8
5	2, 5, 7, 9
6	1, 3, 6, 9
7	1, 2, 4, 8
8	1, 2, 6, 8
9	2, 3, 6, 7

Example: Suppose your date of birth is 14-5-1930. Your marriage will take place during one of those years where the final digit is 2, or 5 or 7 or 9. This year is to be solved as under:

Your Ruling Number	5 (14 = 1 + 4 = 5)
Month of birth	5 (May)
Year of Marriage	1954
Total	1964 = 20 = 2

If the marriage does not take place in 1954, it will take place in other years where the single digit will be 5, 7 or 9.

Late Marriage Or No Marriage

I have sorted out birth dates of those persons who have either late marriage or no marriage at all. Therein also I have arrived at the conclusion that the presence of numbers 8, 3, 6 and 9 in a birth date indicates difficulties in getting married. In this case you have to arrive at the single digit in the date, the month and the year of birth. I give below some dates and their digits which will clarify what I say:

Birth date	*Single Digits*
(1) 27-6-1958	9 - 6 - 5
(2) 29-9-1959	2 - 9 - 6
(3) 19-6-1956	1 - 6 - 3
(4) 12-2-1959	3 - 2 - 6
(5) 8-7-1952	8 - 7 - 8
(6) 17-3-1923	8 - 3 - 6

You will find that in the above birth-dates, there is a combination of numbers 3, 6 and 9. These numbers may occur in any serial in a birth-date. Atleast two of these three numbers are present in the birth-date. At some spaces, the number 8 which shows delay is also present.

The above observation is found in about 30% cases. Even after the marriage, some marital problems are experienced.

Suppose you receive your friends who have marital problems and no compatibility, you can study their birth-dates and also their names. If the birth-date shows compatibility, but even then the two are not happy in their married life and have clashes on small matters, you can work out the vowels in their names and suggest a change in their names so that at least on the mental level there is harmony. For making such a change, refer to the chapter 16, 'What's in a name'"

I do hope this chapter will be useful when the time comes for you to choose your partner in marriage. You should do it by selecting the correct period of birth date of your partner or by making a change either in your name or that of your partner.

CHAPTER 28

WORLD PEACE THROUGH NUMEROLOGY

In this book you have studied that the 'Theory of Numerology is based on vibrations which are emitted either through the birth date or the name of an individual. You have also studied the significance of numbers 1 to 9 and also of the alphabets A to Z. In the last chapter, you studied how you can make a choice of your marriage partner. The study of numerology is basically a study of psycho-analysis. You can extend this theory further and apply it to different nations and their leaders. From such a study, you will be able to find out the harmony or repulsion between two countries or two leaders. If the leaders of the world try to understand other nations and their leaders through the psycho-analysis given by numbers, there is a possibility of achieving harmony between them whereby world tension can be minimized and world peace is possible. You can try for world peace on the following basis.

Choice Of A Proper Vocation

Practically every individual is unhappy about his job. This is because of selection of a wrong profession. If from the birth-date you can suggest and recommend a suitable vocation, he can avoid clashes with his superiors and get the job satisfaction. That would make him peaceful and enjov his life and have harmonious relations with his family members and neighbors. That would create a serene atmosphere around him.

Health is Wealth: (Healthy mind in a healthy body)

Health is a precious thing. Numerology helps you to know your physical as well as your mental weakness. If you try to overcome these weaknesses, life is smooth and you can lead a happy life. If your health is sound, the mind is sound. Thus you can understand others better if your mind is at peace.

Name Vibrations

You have studied the vibrations of the alphabets A to Z and consequently the vibrations of a name. Every letter has a sound and therefore a name emits sound vibrations. You can analyse vibrations and work out the characteristics of that person. This is equally applicable to the names of the country as well as to the cities. The name of a city creates certain vibrations and the people living in that city have a particular psychological pattern. People living in London have a particular behaviour, likes and dislikes. Similarly, people in Delhi, Bombay, Tokyo and other cities of the world also have their own psychological make up which you will study later. Once you know the mental condition or behaviour of people living in a particular country or city, you know very well how to adjust with them. This is how you can create harmony and friendship with other people and cities and countries can come together and live in harmony.

Will It Not Help World Peace:

You will now study the names of few cities according to the numbers allotted to their alphabets.

London: 1 + 7 + 5 + 4 + 7 + 5 = 31 = 3 + 1 = 4

The psychological vibrations of the city of London are that of the number 4 which is governed by the planet, Harshal. Therefore the people living in London have originality, activity and they are reliable, methodic and systematic. Their drawbacks are stubbornness and domination.

Berlin = 2 + 5 + 2 + 3 + 1 + 5 = 18 = 1 + 8 = 9

The psychological vibrations of the city of Berlin are that of the number 9 which is governed by the planet Mars. Therefore the people living in Berlin are warriors. They have courage, dash and enthusiasm. Their drawbacks are that they are hot-tempered, impatient and quarrelsome.

Tokyo = 4 + 7 + 2 + 1 + 7 = 21 = 2 + 1 = 3

The psychological vibrations of the city of Tokyo are that of the number 3 which is governed by the planet Jupiter. People living in Tokyo have a sense of morality, and justice, and they adore pure love. Their drawbacks are vanity, cruelty and hypocrisy.

Delhi = 4 + 5 + 3 + 5 + 1 = 18 = 1 + 8 = 9

The significance of Delhi is the same as that of Berlin.

America = 1 + 4 + 5 + 2 + 1 + 3 + 1 = 17 = 1 + 7 = 8

The number 8 is governed by the planet Saturn and shows authority, method, steadiness and system. The drawbacks are cynicism, nervousness, delay and vindictiveness.

Bharat = 2 + 5 + 1 + 2 + 1 + 4 = 15 = 1 + 5 = 6

India = 1 + 5 + 4 + 1 + 1 = 12 = 1 + 2 = 3

Likewise, we can work out the psychological make-up of the people living in different countries and the cities. Once we know their psychological behaviour, it is easy to adjust with them and have a cooperative approach.

From the above discussions, it will be clear that every city or country has an overall psychological impact on the individuals living in that city. That is why we say. "This is characteristic of the people of Delhi or those of Bombay people or London". In general, their patterns of thinking, living and acting depends much on the vibrations they live in. In addition, every individual has his own vibrations, thinking and behaviour.

Now we shall study some countries and their leaders.

U. S. S. R. = 14 = 5

MIKHAIL GORBACHEV

17 + 34 = 51 = 6

The country U.S.S.R. is represented by No. 5 and the planet Mercury. Therefore the people living in Russia are intelligent, scientific minded and most practical. The name "Mikhail" is dominated by number 8 which is governed by Saturn and shows seriousness, discipline, system, and methods. The vibration of the name "Gorbachev" are 34, i.e. 7, which number is dominated by the planet Neptune. It shows idealism, peace, reflection, tolerance etc. The total vibrations of the name when reduced to single digit are 6. This number represents Venus, a planet of love, cooperation, harmony and peace. Due to the numbers shown by U.S.S.R. and her leader, there is no doubt that Russia will help to create world peace.

Pakistan	=	25	=	7
Benazir	=	23	=	5
Bhutto	=	28	=	1

The vibrations of the total name of Benazir Bhutto work out to 6 (5 + 1). We have seen above that Mikhail Gorbachev also represents number 6. Therefore these two countries may work together in the future. The vibrations of Bharat or India are also 6 and 3. It means India will also cultivate good relations with Russia. In short, there is every possibility that India,

Pakistan and Russia may join hands to create world peace.

England	=	26	=	8
5533154				
Margaret	=	22	=	4
41231254				
Thatcher	=	29	=	2
45143552				

We notice that England and America are both governed by the number 8 showing conservatism. They will always stay together. The name Mikhail also represents 8. Therefore America and England will appreciate the policies of Mr. Mikhail Gorbachev. The total name vibrations of the Russian Prime Minister are 6 i.e. the same as that of Margaret Thatcher (4 + 2). It shows that the British Prime Minister and the Russian Prime Minister have a natural affinity towards each other.

In conclusion, we may say that the Eastern Block represented by Russia, India and Pakistan will be very powerful and the Western Block represented by England and America will also be cooperative and will come together to achieve world peace.

BIBLIOGRAPHY

1. The Kabala of Numbers — Sepharial
2. The Number of book — Sepharial
3. Cheiro's Book of Numbers — Cheiro
4. Your Destiny in Numbers — P. N. Scherman
5. Birth Day Numerology — Manik Chand Jain
6. Numerollogy for Everybody — Montrose
7. The Essentials of Numerololgy — Narendra Desai
8. Numerology — Austin Coates
9. Modern Numerology — Morris C. Goodman
10. Numerology—Its Facts and Secrets — Ariel Y. Taylor
11. Numerology (True Facts of Numbers)— Pandit Lakshmi Doss
12. Modern Numerology — T. V. Rajagopal
    R. B. Shastri
13. A Treatise on Predictive Numerology — B. J. Rao
14. Numerology in a Nutshell — Rasajo
15. Know your Future through Your Birth Date — Shiraz
16. The Secrets of Numerology — B. S. Sekhar
17. Numerology for All — Pandit Ashutosh Ojha
18. How to Apply Numerology — James Leigh